JERSEY UNDER THE
JACKBOOT

JERSEY UNDER THE JACKBOOT

R. C. F. Maugham
C.B.E., F.R.G.S., F.Z.S.

NEW ENGLISH LIBRARY

First published in Great Britain in 1946 by W. H. Allen & Co. Ltd

First NEL Paperback Edition June 1980
Reprinted April 1984
Reprinted June 1985

NEL Books are published by
New English Library,
Mill Road, Dunton Green,
Sevenoaks, Kent.
Editorial office: 47 Bedford Square, London WC1B 3DP

Printed and bound in Great Britain by
Hunt Barnard Printing Ltd., Aylesbury, Bucks.

0 450 04714 8

I dedicate this book, in deep and abiding sympathy, to many hundreds of dauntless English and Scottish-born subjects of His Majesty, torn from their homes in Jersey on a sadly memorable day of September 1942 and consigned to a devitalising, nerve-shattering existence in the loathsome squalor of Continental German prison camps.

All honour to them for their unshakable fortitude at that the bitterest, most heartbreaking moment of their lives.

PREFACE

In the making of this book I have yielded to the oft-repeated requests of many persons both English and Jersey born. During the years of the German Occupation of Jersey, with my long-suffering wife, I remained to all intents and purposes a prisoner of war in the Island and was thus a witness of much that I have sought in the following pages to set down and to describe. My task has not been an agreeable one, for, truth to tell, I have found but little of an agreeable character for my pen to record.

During the fifteen years of my residence in Jersey, I have seen the Island at the height of its happiness and prosperity, a prosperity which it is struggling to regain; but I fear that years must elapse before anything resembling outstanding success will crown such efforts.

Up to the end of 1939 Jersey had become, in the course of the years, a haven of refuge for many hundreds of persons who had settled there at the end of successful, often distinguished, careers in the service of the Crown, in the professions, and in the world of business. These people had been attracted to the Island by its genial climate, its low taxation, its general comparative inexpensiveness, and by the tranquillity which, after a life of activity, Jersey seemed to offer. These advantages, on the whole, were largely realised. Life in the Island was pleasant and peaceful; English residents occupied for the most part comfortable, well-equipped houses surrounded by charming gardens and grounds. They kept smart motor cars, and exercised to the full, year in and year out, a delightful, open-handed hospitality which, beyond all question, went far to place the small Island in a class by iself. There was everything to do that any reasonable person could possibly wish to do, and the years passed quickly—for many people, indeed, all too quickly.

Then came the war, the flight of great numbers of English residents, the German Occupation and, finally, after five long years of misery, privation and incredible suffering, our liberation.

Thereafter, as opportunity grudgingly offered, evacuated families began slowly to make their way back, but, to their anguish and dismay, it was to a Jersey different indeed from the small Island which, in the years that had gone before, they had grown so intimately to know and so deeply to love.

6

Some found on arrival that their homes had completely disappeared; others that, while the almost unrecognisable shell of their premises remained, their household goods and effects had completely vanished. A fortunate few, and they were very few, whose houses had been occupied by German officers of high rank, found that they had sustained but little in the way of spoliation or loss. But the great majority spent many distracted days and weeks in gradually and bitterly learning the worst.

They were not long, moreover, in discovering that Jersey's greatest and most valued advantages had likewise disappeared: house-rent and living costs had vastly increased, so had taxation, all wages had doubled, domestic help was practically unobtainable, few hotels were in a condition to receive them, and such as had found means to open their doors were filled with stranger guests. Other accommodation was difficult, almost impossible to find, for numbers of persons, knowing little or nothing of the Island but thankful to escape at the earliest possible moment from unbearable conditions in the United Kingdom, had flocked to Jersey and had snapped up, at enormously inflated prices, such habitable houses as they found available or such lodgings as could take them in. Gradually hopeful anticipation gave way to a sense of frustration and disillusionment, and not a few of the old residents quitted the Island once more in despair.

Returning ex-Servicemen and people of the poorer classes of the 1940 evacuees could find no homes at all – not even a humble cottage to shelter them. They had perforce to be lodged and boarded in more or less unsuitable buildings at the cost of the Island Administration.

The foregoing picture is one which, at the time of writing, a full year after its liberation, the Island of Jersey presents to returning residents and to the many who, ignorant of actual conditions, are now hopefully making their way there.

While the offices of the local Treasury are choked with claims for war-damage and loss, the States Assembly, all prematurely, is straining every effort to attract tourists and holiday-makers for whom the Island is still scarcely ready. Almost every issue of the local Press contains well-founded complaints from persons who in some cases have failed to obtain reasonable accommodation and have left the Island, while letters published from returning demobilised soldiers bitterly enquire if the wretched plight in which they and their families find themselves is their reward for all they have suffered and for which they fought. In this respect, at any rate, the situation in Jersey closely resembles that in the United Kingdom.

Whether Jersey is likely in the future to live again the happy,

7

care-free years to which before 1940 the islanders and residents had grown so blissfully accustomed, seems doubtful. Much careful planning will have to be undertaken and much hard work done before the people can hope once more to enjoy anything even remotely resembling the easy prosperity which they experienced in the long dead days before the war. In such planning and work Jersey statesmen have their opportunity. Will they rise to the occasion?

R. C. F. MAUGHAM.

Spring Bank, Jersey (1946).

CHAPTER ONE

HOW WAR CAME TO JERSEY

THE impact of war upon the small Island of Jersey was considerably softened by the gradualness of its onset. From September 1939 to the following June life went on from day to day very much as before. Mail steamers arrived from British ports bringing passengers, cargo of all descriptions, letters and newspapers. Our wireless receiving sets provided daily details of what seemed the amazingly slow progress of the conflict. Deeply distressed as we were by our grievous losses at sea, we retained, nevertheless, unshakable confidence in the impregnability of the Maginot Line, and in the steadfast resolution of the French and Belgian armies.

Those of us who had lived in Jersey during the 1914–18 war regarded the future with almost complete equanimity. They recalled that at no time during those years was the life of the Island in any material manner disturbed or affected. Beyond the fact that prices increased, the war made little or no difference. Food was plentiful, crops were harvested in their due season, journeys to the Mainland were undertaken as occasion arose and travellers returned in perfect safety. Large profits were made by tradesmen and farmers, the food of the people cost them more, which, of course, was to be expected. That, practically speaking, was the only inconvenience that Jersey suffered, and those who could look back and remember were firmly convinced that history would repeat itself.

But history did not repeat itself.

First came the rude shock of the Belgian submission, for which nothing had prepared the minds of the Jersey public. Belgium, it had been felt, might be relied upon to fight on to the end. The Belgian Army, which, in the last war, inspired by its heroic King, had opposed to the German onslaught a gallant resistance, had now the support of the British and French forces, and, to us living in Jersey at any rate, no thought or anticipation of so shattering and far-reaching a disaster had ever, even remotely, occurred. The splendid withdrawal and escape of great masses of the British army from Dunkirk was breathlessly followed, and still our confidence in the ability of the French to hold out until we could re-organise remained unabated. Of their whole-hearted devotion to the Allied cause no shadow of doubt for one moment entered into our minds. That they would resist to the death the ignominy and humiliation of another German invasion of the fair land of France seemed an unquestionable and unshakable certainty. The French armies, as it was understood, were of such strength and so perfectly equipped as to be able safely to cope with any eventuality.

There was, moreover, the Maginot Line and although, due to querulous Belgian objection, that great bulwark had not been extended along the Franco—Belgian frontier, it was confidently expected to afford almost complete protection elsewhere. Oh, yes, people said, France would be well able to keep the German columns in check until a re-formed, re-equipped British Expeditionary Force could go once more to her assistance. We deplored the disaster; but were not unduly shaken by it. The end was not in doubt. The Belgian *débâcle*, while certainly a grave misfortune, was only one of those unforeseen happenings incidental to war which, as everyone knew, could never be regarded as an exact science.

But, as the days passed, they brought us little ground for maintained confidence. We were told of an ominous bulge in the French battle front; of its gradual extension; of the falling back of the flanks to restore the line; of bridges which should have been blown up but had not been blown up; of the replacement, during the fighting, of army corps and divisional commanders, and of other disquieting happenings for which nothing had prepared us.

Then, on an unforgettable Sunday morning in that fateful but lovely June, came the first incredible whisper that France had asked for terms of capitulation. As the day wore on, the fell rumour was amply confirmed. We looked at each other blankly in the face, dumb with anguish and apprehension. One thing was abundantly and disquietingly clear: the defection of France had left Great Britain to face alone the entire weight of the mighty German war machine. We had not a single friend in arms to help us.

The German terms were communicated, and France, proud France, laid down her arms.

With the French Channel Ports and Atlantic Coast now firmly in the hands of the enemy, Jersey, Guernsey and Alderney, with the smaller islands of the group, could look forward to one thing and one thing only, namely a speedy German Occupation. For this, there were obviously a number of reasons. First and foremost, in the Teutonic mind, came the glory and prestige of being able to boast that the Nazi Flag flew over British Possessions. That they were insignificantly tiny Possessions mattered not at all. At last, at long last and for the first time, the German Jackboot was to plant itself on British soil. Here was something tangible; a first step towards the final disruption of the British Empire which Hitler had sworn to accomplish; something that the German Wireless Station, with appropriate musical accompaniment, could blare forth to a wildly enthusiastic German people. It was to be the beginning of the end of Britain; the prelude to the intended invasion of the United Kingdom which, in its successful achievement, an achievement which no son of the Fatherland for one moment doubted, would crown with success the deeply-laid ambitious designs of the unconquerable Rome–Berlin Axis and, as its sequel, give to Nazi Germany, led by Hitler, the unchallengeable dictatorship of Europe and, later doubtless, of the entire world. World-wide dominion foreshadowed by the bold German occupation of the British Channel Islands!

But there was even more in it than that. The islands would prove useful submarine bases for the destruction of British shipping. They possessed admirably laid out airports. Planes based upon them could keep ceaseless watch over the Channel and search the waters, even of the Atlantic itself, for vessels to attack and destroy. Were any further inducement lacking, German cupidity was stirred by the information of considerable wealth, in various forms, which the small islands contained; of the valuable property of wealthy inhabitants, and the contents of the vaults of half a dozen important banks. There was certainly ample inducement.

Meanwhile, greatly perturbed, the anxious Jersey people and the equally disquieted residents, awaited with unconcealed misgiving what the future might hold for them. Many, without loss of time, quitted the Island; but the great majority held back until the arrival of some authoritative disclosure of the intentions of His Majesty's Government. Would the Island be defended? That was the vital question which exercised all minds.

In the meantime, the Jersey States Authorities, faced for the first time by problems of unexampled magnitude and complexity, lived from day to day in a condition of nervous uncertainty. Meeting after meeting took place. The harassed chairman of the Committee of Island Defence propounded and carried into effect without let or hindrance (for nobody knew what steps to take) such immediate precautionary measures as commended themselves to him. As the result of such measures, a number of perfectly harmless old gentlemen, who would have been much better in bed, spent many hours nightly, in all weathers, guarding gasometers, reservoirs, electrical generating stations and other insular and municipal undertakings from—they knew not what! A body of men largely drawn, I believe, from the Jersey Militia and the ranks of the British Legion were placed under the command of long-retired, somewhat aged army officers and drafted to various so-called keypoints or danger-zones into which the Island was divided. These men, I am told, apart from the Militia, were armed with a variety of miscellaneous firearms, but what orders they received, or what they were instructed to do with their weapons, I never learned, and I consider it extremely doubtful if they did. In any case, they certainly did not spare themselves, and I feel sure that, in so far as they understood them, they carried out their duties conscientiously to the end.

12

About this time, although no food shortage was yet discernible, ration books were issued to the general public. These had been prepared some weeks previously by a band of voluntary workers recruited from among ladies and men of the leisured classes who worked for several months and for many hours daily not only on the preparation of these documents but on the card-indexing of the entire Island population—no light task.

On Wednesday, June 19th, the long-expected decision of His Majesty's Government to demilitarise the Island of Jersey was formally announced by the Lieutenant-Governor, Major-General J. H. R. Harrison, C.B., at a special meeting of the States.

His Excellency stated that, at a recent secret session of that body, he had already informed members of the gravity of the situation. Since then, in so far as these Islands were concerned, evacuation of British troops arriving from Cherbourg and St. Malo had been effectively carried out. He had received orders to embark all troops in Jersey, and this was proceeding. He went on to say that, as demilitarisation of the Island was a probability, this would mean the evacuation and disbandment of all military bodies, including local defence forces. The Home Government scheme for evacuation included all those who might desire to leave, but, added the Lieutenant-Governor, he felt sure that those who had their roots in the soil would wish to remain. He himself might be compelled to leave, in which case the Bailiff would carry on his duties. The future was hidden from them; but they had to act quickly, and that was his reason for convening the House which would have to discuss the question of the evacuation of those who wished to leave the Island which would, of course, be defenceless. It might be occupied; His Majesty's Government hoped that it would not be; but they could rest assured that such *occupation would not be of long duration.*

The Bailiff (Mr. A. M. Coutanche) stated that a Mr. Dorey had proceeded to England in his (the speaker's) place, and was expected back that evening. He hoped that, for the forthcoming evacuation, ships would be available for the large

13

number of persons desirous of going. A great number had booked to leave, and it was possible that accommodation for all would not be available. Mr. Dorey, on his return, would communicate the English scheme, but the Island would be responsible for those who were without funds to take them away. Steps would at once be taken to effect registration of these latter, which would be undertaken by a central authority. Continuing, the speaker said: 'As regards the evacuation, no one would care to accept the responsibility of advising any one else, but, if there was not enough room, they should follow the old rule of the sea, *Women and children first.*' He thought it would be only right to make provision for men of military age. It would be appropriate, therefore, that men between the ages of 20 and 33 should place themselves on the transporting ships. If the Island was to be demilitarised as had been foreshadowed, the armed forces of the Crown, including the Militia, would go.

A few minutes later, the Lieutenant-Governor again rose and stated that, but a moment before, he had received a message from the War Office to the effect that the Cabinet had decided on the complete demilitarisation of the Island of Jersey, whereupon——

The House unanimously decided to authorise the implementing of arrangements for evacuation already made.

It was announced in the Island Press that shipping facilities for evacuation were being provided by His Majesty's Government. Notice was to be given, at the Town Hall, St. Helier, that night (June 19th) or the following day.

There was a rush to register. On that memorable evening and far into the night long queues of silent, pale-faced people formed up intent upon one thing only, to get their names upon the list. The following morning, at an early hour and throughout the day, the Town Hall was almost unapproachable, and now the local crowd was reinforced by many from the country districts. Nothing like it had ever been witnessed before in Jersey. The people were quiet and well conducted; terror and anxiety fought for expression upon their pallid faces. Quietly they received their registration coupons and hurried away to

14

their homes to make arrangements to leave.

On Thursday, June 20th, the Bailiff issued a Proclamation signed by himself and all the members of the States which it was hoped would have a calming effect. It was in the following terms:

'At this anxious hour, we wish the people of this Island to know, for their guidance and assistance in the decision which each must take for himself and his own, that we are remaining at our posts to carry out our respective duties, and that we are all of us who have them or either of them keeping with us our wives and families.'

But, to all appearances, the harm had unfortunately been done. The phrase in the Bailiff's speech wherein he pleaded for priority for the women and children had swept like a sandstorm through the Island.

Later in the day, at another emergency meeting of the States Assembly, the Bailiff communicated to the House the first knowledge of conditions in the country districts stating that panic-stricken farmers were turning their cattle loose in the fields and preparing to burn their crops.

Members present informed the House that, in other cases, farmers had locked up their live-stock and were fleeing from their homes, conduct which was severely reprobated, although the reason for it was, of course, well understood.

The Bailiff then proceeded to make a solemn declaration that the States of Jersey would repay to His Majesty's Government all monies expended on the evacuation of persons from Jersey to British ports.

The Constable of St. Helier thereupon furnished the number of applicants for evacuation up to that morning as follows:

Those who undertook to pay their passages or with homes or friends to go to	3,480
Those who applied to travel free	4,861
Men between 20 and 33 years of age	434
Total	8,775

(By June 21st, however, persons registered reached a total of 23,062. Finally, the number actually to leave the Island reached a figure between ten and eleven thousand.)

Mr. Dorey, who had returned from London on the previous day, then spoke of his experience at the Home Office. He had all along, he said, realised that there were persons who had interest in England who might wish to leave, or young men who might be desirous of joining up, and these were persons worthy of careful consideration. 'But,' speaking with great warmth and excitement, he added, 'this morning I have been filled with disgust. I could understand some people being desirous of going, but I do not understand those of old Norman stock, who should be rooted in the soil, pressing to leave. We, who were always a calm, steady people, have jogged along in our own way loving our lands and our surroundings. I would like the House to express its utter contempt at what these people are doing. I have spoken to a few in language which I could not use in this House. This is worse than folly; it is the worst characteristic in human nature, cowardice. Clearly the young men should be got away. They should be sent on a separate boat, and should not be herded with the rabbits and rats that are leaving otherwise.'

On the same day, the Bailiff delivered a series of brief speeches, both in the Royal Square and elsewhere. He implored the people to keep calm. He assured his not always very patient hearers that he and his colleagues would not leave the Island and would do all in their power to safeguard the islanders' interests and rights. Mr. Coutanche's speeches were doubtless intended to have a tranquillising effect; but it would have required more than a few words which on each occasion he uttered to allay the mass hysteria which already had the whole Island in its grip.

On Friday, June 21st, the Bailiff was sworn as temporary Lieutenant-Governor, and Major-General Harrison left for England. A translation of the Bailiff's oath will be found in the Appendix.

It was reported in the Press that more than half of the population of the Island had registered for evacuation. This

16

fact may afford some explanation of the warmth of Mr. Dorey's remarks in the States Assembly. But the town of St. Helier continued in a state of uproar. Shipping offices were besieged. Crowds thronged the streets. The most terrifying rumours passed rapidly from group to group. As the day advanced, hundreds of men, women and children, the aged, the halt and the infirm, converged upon the town. 'Do you think we shall get away in time?' 'When do you think the Germans will come?' 'They say their bombers may be here any minute.' 'I was told that reconnoitring planes were over this morning.' Such were the questions and statements bandied about. St. Helier was packed with people from all parts of the Island, many of whom had already abandoned their houses and belongings and hastened in to the port intent on finding shipping room of any kind, even on deck or down in the hold.

There was a formidable run on the Banks. From the door of each, controlled by Police, long queues of anxious-eyed persons five and six deep, extended. Maximum withdrawals were perforce fixed at twenty-five pounds. Had it not been for this prudent limitation, it is possible that cash resources might have proved insufficient. St. Helier possesses five branches of the Great London Banks, and also a local Savings Bank. The experience of all was the same. The harassed bank officials worked feverishly; closing time was extended, but demands of the public for funds to enable them to depart were so insistent that, hours before doors were opened in the mornings, long columns of nervous customers had already formed and lengthened still more as the day wore on. Great credit is due to the Jersey Banks for the patience and courtesy which they displayed in dealing with a situation of unparalleled difficulty.

At length came the hour of departure. At the head of each jetty barricades had been erected at which officials examined evacuation permits, but already hundreds of depressed-looking people, many apparently possessed of but little in the way of personal belongings, thronged the piers. Throughout the previous night some had slept there on the stone pavement, huddled together in a promiscuity far more dreadful to witness than the packed deck passengers on a Mecca-Pilgrimage

17

steamer in the Red Sea. Many had never before left the Island. With their wailing infants and older children, provided with small, hopelessly insufficient supplies of food and water for the voyage, they sat patiently with husbands and parents and relatives through the long hours of that burning midsummer day. As time wore on, more and still more people came to increase the throngs on the already overcrowded piers. Finally, they were at length permitted to make their way on board the squalid, uninviting vessels which awaited them. These consisted of small colliers and potato boats. It has been stated that certain other and more suitable craft had been despatched from England for the purpose but, arrived off Jersey and Guernsey, they received a signal that they were not required and returned empty to their port of departure.

On the small, unbelievably dirty vessels, the desponding passengers were directed to settle themselves down upon the decks and hatches in the open air.

None of these small vessels was designed or intended for the transport of passengers on such a scale or anything like it. The sufferings, therefore, of those unfortunates, packed together almost without room to move, many in the grip of sea-sickness, do not bear contemplation.

The voyage, to several different British ports, was not a short one. The speed of the small craft could not possibly have exceeded seven or eight knots—that of some certainly less. The plight of the unhappy passengers on arrival in England, therefore, must have been a truly sorry one.

But the port of St. Helier, during the embarkation, described and afterwards, presented an unwonted appearance. Numbers of the passengers had driven into the town at the last moment, and abandoned their cars on the jetty. A young clerk standing watching the exodus was presented by its feverishly hurrying owner with a practically new Daimler coupé. The following day, all the abanodned motor-cars, together with many motor-bicycles, were driven away by the Police to a *dépôt* and found their way ultimately into German possession. As for bicycles, these, hastily discarded, flung away into the hedges and ditches on the outskirts of the town, abandoned in

18

the streets and elsewhere, were to be had almost for asking. Nobody imagined that, ere many months had passed and our motor-cars had been taken from us, the despised 'push-bike' would be changing hands almost for its weight in gold.

If the foregoing affords a dim and imperfect description of the scenes in St. Helier, how were the country districts faring? At a by no means unimportant farm well known to me this is what I found.

A deserted homestead. The panic-stricken family had clearly fled away in a blind, unreasoning scare. Some of the doors were closed, others swinging on their hinges. Peacefully enough, fowls were scratching in the yard, and I could hear the unfed pigs grunting in their sty. Entering the house, I found in the living-room the remains of a hasty meal strewn about on the table. The bedrooms were in disorder. Everything betokened mad haste, precipitate, unreflecting flight, and I could not but share the bitterness of the distracted wife, compelled to leave her home, with all its accumulated treasures, knowing full well that she might never see them again. How this forced abandonment must have pierced the very soul of this home-loving Jersey family! Deeply distressed, I closed the door after me and left the farm-yard, eyeing regretfully the handsome Jersey cattle in an adjoining field as I wondered, helplessly, who would milk them at sunset.

In striking contrast to this dreadful thing that had come upon us, the sweet, unspoiled country was lovely in the soft June evening. Below me, a tiny wooded valley, a fold in a series of smooth undulations, displayed masses of the tender greenery of early summer. The westering sun filtered through thick foliage of splendid oaks and beeches, dappling with golden light the green of the grass beneath. Except for the songs of the birds, there was not a sound to be heard, not a soul to be seen. One sensed, in the brooding silence, the approach of impending disaster, of coming calamity. I turned away and, profoundly saddened, wended my way homeward, wondering apprehensively what the morrow would bring with it for us all.

Unhappily, the little picture which I have tried to paint of an abandoned Jersey homestead was but one of very many which might have been similarly described. Silent tradesmen's shops with their stocks intact; small country inns with nobody behind the bar; petrol pumps derelict and unattended; the roads empty save for a few, a very few old country folk who appeared to be incapable of replying to the simplest question, their minds a blank, their eyes vacantly staring, staring up into the sky. They were all that remained of the populous Parish of yesterday or the day before.

On June 22nd, at an emergency meeting of the States, plans were laid before the House and in principle agreed upon, for the collection and disposal of all property, especially foodstuffs and articles of a perishable character, abandoned in the houses of those who had fled from the Island.

By this time, the establishment of administrative departments, described in another chapter, had been carried into effect. One of the first measures laid before the States at a sitting held on June 27th, was a bill, sponsored by the Department of Agriculture, for the taking over by that body of land and cattle, the property of evacuated persons, such land and cattle to be utilised in the public interest and for the benefit, and at the cost, of the absent owners. This bill passed at once through all its stages, and was doubtless of substantial benefit to everybody concerned.

In the town of St. Helier, although business continued to be carried on, if somewhat mechanically, great uncertainty prevailed. Nobody knew or could foresee what would happen from the moment that control passed, as it was felt it inevitably would pass, into German hands. Such questions as those connected with banking, currency, credit, the positions of persons with fixed pensions or other forms of unvarying income from the moment that communication with the Mainland was completely interrupted, all these and others of a kindred nature remained unanswered and unanswerable. So far as was known the Banks would remain open, unless closed or taken over by the enemy; but for the rest pure surmise reigned and rumoured, growing daily more fantastic, only served to render confusion worse confounded.

On June 24th, however, an admirable letter was published in the local Press. This letter (which will be found in the Appendix at the end of this book) was from the pen of Mr. Trevor J. Matthews, a distinguished financial authority who, fortunately for Jersey, had elected to remain in the Island. In this very far-seeing document Mr. Matthews made a number of valuable suggestions. He pointed out certain errors into which the public, in such conditions as those then prevailing were liable to fall—indeed had already to some extent fallen. It is satisfactory to be able to place on record that effect was speedily given to most if not all of the recommendations which Mr. Matthews made, with advantages which continued to be felt throughout the years of German Occupation. I was informed that Mr. Matthews, with self-sacrificing public spirit, freely and without reward offered to place his unrivalled knowledge and experience, in an advisory capacity, at the service of the States. This proposal the States did not, unhappily, see their way to accept.

But throughout the Island grave anxiety prevailed. It was thought by many that His Majesty's Government had left us to our fate; that, being immersed in matters of greater importance, the welfare of the Channel Islands was no longer regarded in London as of serious moment. The people saw no reason to view the situation with anything even remotely resembling confidence. The Home Government, they felt with bitterness, had failed them.

It was precisely at this juncture, and when feeling was running at its highest—or lowest—that a gracious Message from His Majesty the King was received by the Bailiff and read in the States on June 24th. Although manifestly intended that it should receive the widest publicity, it was, in fact, never published as it should have been, not even in the Press, and thousands of persons who would have derived the utmost encouragement from its contents were ignorant, five years later, of its receipt or even of its existence.

The Message was in the following terms:

'For strategic reasons it has been found necessary to

21

withdraw the armed forces from the Channel Islands.

'I deeply regret this necessity, and I wish to assure my people in the Islands that, in taking this decision, my Government have not been unmindful of their position.

'It is in their interest that this step should be taken in the present circumstances.

'The long association of the Islands with the Crown and the loyal services the people of the Islands have rendered to my ancestors and myself are guarantees that the link between us will remain unbroken, and I know that my people in the Islands will look forward with the same confidence as I do to the day when the resolute fortitude with which we face our present difficulties will reap the reward of victory.

GEORGE R.I.'

Had this message been broadcast to the islanders instead of being merely read to a handful of preoccupied officials, there can be no doubt that the public mind would have been greatly relieved.

June 27th witnessed the first approach of hostile forces.

During the afternoon of that day, aeroplanes flying at a moderate height, their exhausts describing a cryptic series of mysterious loops and figures, were observed in the clear blue of the Summer sky. By some, these planes were hopefully believed to be British, on a visit of encouragement and reassurance; but persons provided with powerful glasses or telescopes had no difficulty in identifying them by their black-cross markings, as unmistakably German. As evening advanced, however, the machines withdrew, leaving the populace nervous, overwrought, greatly fearing for the morrow.

Friday, June 28th, dawned. The brilliant weather continued unbroken. Sea and sky were alike of the deepest blue. It seemed impossible, incredible that, with Nature at her brightest and best, war, with its horror and bestiality, could exist anywhere. The Island lay basking in the sunshine, a paradigm of perfect peace. On that morning, crowded almost beyond capacity, the last mail steamer, transporting the last passengers to leave the Island, left for Guernsey and England.

With her departure, the small port of St. Helier was completely emptied of sea-going shipping; the last link which bound us to the Mother Country was finally broken.

The day passed quietly and without incident. The streets of the town presented an unusually empty appearance. Small groups no longer congregated on the side-walks. Faces of passers-by wore an expression of nervous strain. Glancing occasionally upward, they seemed to be listening for something, perhaps for the growing drone of hostile aircraft. The very beauty of the day appeared, in some mysterious, inexplicable manner, to heighten and accentuate an all-pervading sense of haunting tension. The air teemed with unspoken questions to which nobody knew the answers. People out of doors seemed affected by a deep-rooted, almost subliminal intuition, a brooding sense of the unavoidable approach of coming tragedy.

The brilliant afternoon faded into early evening. The afternoon breeze died away. Suddenly a series of deafening explosions in the port area, followed by the rattle of murderous machine-gun fire, apprised a startled public that their worst fears were at long last realised.

Several German planes, flying low, mercilessly bombed and machine-gunned the helpless, undefended town. The peace of the perfect June evening was shattered. Great columns of smoke, dust and *débris* rose high over the stricken port. To the roar of the explosions was added a series of palpable shocks; buildings trembled and rocked, roofs were shivered and windows splintered over a wide area. A few people were lying here and there; some quite still, others very nearly so, others again rushed wildly for shelter from the machine-gun bullets which rained down upon them, claiming still more victims.

The first bombs had fallen; the first blood had flowed; the first cries of agony had been uttered. The peaceful little town will not soon be as it was an hour ago, for war has branded it with new and indelible scars.

The first explosions were heard from the direction of La Rocq, where several fatal casualties occurred and, as the planes

23

approaching St. Helier passed over Grève d'Azette and Fort Regent, heavy machine-gun fire was opened. Having bombed the port, the aircraft flew on towards Beaumont and St. Aubin where, having fired upon inoffensive wayfarers on the public roads, they turned back and once more directed their fire upon the port and its surroundings. They then flew off, doubtless to send in a flamboyant report of the brilliant air victory which, without loss to themselves, had crowned what they no doubt described as an exploit conceived and carried out in the best traditions of the incomparable German Air Force.

With commendable promptitude the dead, eleven in number, were removed; the injured, ten severely and many less grievously, were conveyed to hospital. A hasty survey of damage to property indicated that a number of buildings overlooking the quays, together with two hotels and many houses, had suffered severely. In other parts of the Island over which the Germans flew, numerous houses, among them a children's Convalescent Home, were struck by bullets, fortunately without loss of life.

June 29th and 30th passed without further attack. On both days enemy aircraft were observed flying over the Island, but these may have been machines sent to reconnoitre, or possibly to photograph the damage wrought. The town and Island resumed, more or less, their normal activities. Horror and anguish at the gratuitous savagery of the useless purposeless outrage were keenly felt and bitterly expressed.

In the early morning hours of Monday, July 1st, sleepers were awakened by a large German aeroplane which roared above St. Helier low over the house roofs. From it were dropped three bags containing copies of an ultimatum in the following terms:

July 1st, 1940

To the Chief of the Military and Civil Authorities, Jersey.

1. I intend to neutralise military establishments in Jersey by occupation.

2. As evidence that the Island will surrender the military and other establishments without resistance and without de-

stroying them, a large white cross is to be shown as follows from 7 a.m., on July 2nd, 1940:

(*a*) in the centre of the Airport in the east of the Island;

(*b*) on the highest point of the fortification of the port;

(*c*) on the square to the north of the inner basin of the harbour.

Moreover, all fortifications, buildings, establishments and houses are to show the white flag.

3. If these signs of peaceful surrender are not observed by 7 a.m., July 2nd, heavy bombardment will take place;

(*a*) against all military objects;

(*b*) against all establishments and objects useful for defence.

4. The signs of surrender must remain up to the time of the occupation of the Island by German troops.

5. Representatives of the Authorities must stay at the Airport until the occupation.

6. All radio traffic and other communication with Authorities outside the Island will be considered hostile action and will be followed by bombardment.

7. Every hostile action against my representatives will be followed by bombardment.

8. In case of peaceful surrender, the lives, property and liberty of peaceful inhabitants are solemnly guaranteed.

(Signed)   The Commander of

The German Air Forces in Normandy.

On the afternoon of the same day, German officers and troops under a certain Captain Gussek arrived by plane at the Island Airport and were met by States Representatives who at once surrendered Jersey. From that moment the Island passed under German occupation.

The foregoing represents the facts. A description of the occupation of Jersey, as it was given to the German Public, will be found in the Appendix.

The first indication of the occupation was the spectacle, late on that Monday afternoon, of troops in field-grey uniforms, mounted on motor-bicycles, and officers in motor-cars proceeding from the Airport in the direction of St. Helier. Arrived in the town, the Post Office, Telephone Exchange, Town Hall and several other buildings were at once placed under guard. Billeting was speedily carried out, various hotels being taken over for the purpose, the populace looked on calmly, sadly, but without disorder of any kind. It is only fair to state that, in their contact and conversations with the States officials, German officers displayed courtesy and tact and, generally speaking, relations between them and the islanders were almost cordial, an attitude which eventually afforded the latter considerable relief.

The following day, the Royal Square and its approaches were thronged by Jersey people of both sexes witnessing, with gloomy, fatalistic interest, the spectacle of German officers entering and leaving the States building, while groups of grey-clad soldiery, slouching about the streets in their heavy, clumping boots, gazed with undisguised astonishment at the doubtless novel and unexpected appearance of the well- and plentifully-stocked tradesmen's shops, displaying, as they did, a profusion of goods of every description. It was a spectacle which, for nigh on two hundred years, Jersey people had been spared; it was one, they felt, which they could well have been spared now. There was no emotion; scarcely any comment, but much deeply felt if inarticulate bitterness. Their Island was theirs no longer. That was the reflection which drove the iron deep into their souls when once the nightmare unreality of the tragic situation finally and forcefully came home to them. The enemy was not at their gates; he was firmly established in their midst, and they were experiencing, although they knew it not yet, the first lightly applied pressure of the crushing German Jackboot.

It was frequently said in England, and not seldom in Jersey, that we in that island had much to be thankful for. Had we? I wonder. You may grow more or less accustomed, after a time no doubt, to the nightly radiance of searchlights and the explosion of near-by bombs. The discharge of anti-aircraft guns may, after more or less experience of them, become a mere boresome interruption of the conversation or occupation of the moment. You may become philosophically tolerant of tiresome if necessary A.R.P. Regulations which may subvert or modify your more ingrained habits. But, with all that, people in England, with a sufficiency of food, never experienced stark want, the almost intolerable pangs of unappeasable hunger, the uncontrollable shiver of unalleviable, bitter cold. Britons on the mainland never had to undergo the soul-searing ignominy of rubbing shoulders with hordes of the well-nourished enemy troops who had caused it all. They did not have their houses, motor-cars, radio sets, firearms and furniture calmly appropriated, their fields laid waste, their crops wantonly destroyed or looted, their roads cut to pieces by steel caterpillar wheels, their men arrested and imprisoned on frivolous charges or no charges at all, their women and girls debauched by a salacious enemy soldiery. They were spared all that and much more. In Jersey we were spared none of those things. Who should have been the more thankful? Again I wonder.

On July 2nd, 1940, the German Commander set up his office at the Town Hall in St. Helier, which mounted a steel-helmeted sentry and displayed an immense German flag complete with a vast black swastika on a white field. A similar flag flew from the flagstaff on the summit of Fort Regent overlooking the town and port. Throughout the day, more and still more troops arrived in the Island. In the course of the afternoon, the first Orders of the Commandant of the Occupation Forces were published in the local Press and placarded in the streets and parishes.

It ran as follows:

1. All inhabitants must be indoors by 11 p.m., and must not leave their homes before 5 a.m.

2. We will respect the population of Jersey, but should anyone attempt to cause trouble, serious measures will be taken.

3. All orders given by the Military Authority are to be strictly obeyed.

4. All spirits must be locked up immediately, and no spirits may be supplied, obtained or consumed henceforth.

This prohibition does not apply to stocks in private houses.

5. No person shall enter the Aerodrome at St. Peter's.

6. All rifles, air-guns, revolvers, daggers, sporting guns and all other weapons whatsoever, except souvenirs, must, together with all ammunition, be delivered at the Town Arsenal by 12 noon to-morrow, July 3rd.

7. All British sailors, airmen and soldiers on leave, including officers in the Island, must report at the Commandant's office, Town Hall, at 10 a.m. to-morrow, July 3rd.

8. No boat or vessel of any description, including any fishing boat, shall leave the harbour or any other place where the same is moored without an order from the Military Authority, to be obtained at the Commandant's Office, Town Hall. All boats arriving in Jersey must remain in harbour until permitted by the Military Commandant to leave. The crew will remain on board. The master will report to the Harbour Master of St. Helier, and will obey his instructions.

9. The sale of motor-spirit is prohibited except for use on essential services such as doctor's vehicles, the delivery of food-stuffs and the Sanitary Services when such vehicles are in possession of Permits from the Military Authority to obtain supplies. The use of cars for private purposes is forbidden.

10. The Black-Out Regulations in force must be obeyed as before.

11. Banks and shops will be open as before.

12. In order to conform with Central European time, all watches and clocks must be advanced one hour at 11 p.m. to-night.

13. It is forbidden to listen to Wireless Transmitting Stations except German and German-controlled Stations.

14. The raising of prices of commodities is forbidden.

(Signed)
The German Commandant of the Island of Jersey.

These orders, in the unmethodical, haphazard lack of any

attempt at correlative arrangement, rather suggests a desire on the part of the newly appointed Commandant to impose inhibitory restrictions of some kind upon the public in order to prepare their minds for others of greater stringency. Captain Gussek was young for a post of responsibility; and it may well have been that he did not quite know how to approach the first administrative task entrusted to him. The result was a curious, miscellaneous jumble which would appear to have been jotted down at odd moments as the various details suggested themselves to him.

In any case, the curtailment of the public's liberties implicit in these Orders, if it did not provoke much comment, was, nevertheless, keenly felt. Especially was this the case in relation to the ban of listening in to the B.B.C. No longer might we hear the well-remembered resounding tones of Big Ben, or the pleasantly modulated voice announcing 'This is London Calling.' Here was an Order which brought home to the least sentient among us a fuller realisation of the fact that we were cut off indeed.

I cannot remember to have heard how many officers and men of the Services were actually caught in Jersey by the occupying German troops; I do not think there were very many. In due course, they were moved to the Continent where, no doubt, they languished as prisoners of war. It does not redound much to the credit of the War Department that some among these men, on leave of absence, had only landed in the Island a day or two before the arrival of the enemy forces. At the time their leave was granted His Majesty's Government must have known perfectly well that Jersey was already demilitarised, and that, as a consequence, its occupation was imminent.

On July 8th, a lengthy additional list of Orders was published. These included an acknowledgement of the 'loyal co-operation of the Civil Authorities,' recognised the continuance by the States of the Civil Government of the Island conditionally upon good behaviour, but demanded submission to the German Authorities, before enactment, of all future Laws, Ordinances, Regulations and Orders. It empowered the Island Court to deal with and punish offenders except those punishable by German Military Law. It permitted Divine Service and prayers for the British Royal Family and State, church bells being run ten minutes only before services. No assembly was to be made the medium for propaganda or utterances offensive to the German Government or Forces. Cinemas and other forms of entertainment were permitted with a similar restriction. Rigid precautions against drunkenness were prescribed, and the Rate of Exchange was provisionally fixed at eight Reichsmarks to the pound sterling.

On and from July 13th, German currency in the form of paper Reichsmarks poured into Jersey, the values being R.M. 20, 5, 2, 1 and 50 pfennigs. The Exchange Rate was altered to seven Reichsmarks to the pound.

By the end of July 1940, British silver currency was rapidly disappearing from circulation, and although Treasury notes of the one pound and ten shilling values remained, business began to feel the effect of the scarcity of small change. In these conditions, the Reichsmark gradually came into daily use, complication arising from the instability of the Exchange Rate which, as will have been seen, had already twice undergone alteration in the short space of a month. What had become of the British silver nobody seemed to know; even the banks could offer no explanation.

That, to a great extent, its disappearance was due to hoarding by unreflecting Jersey people there can be little doubt; but that it was also collected and exported by Germans in large amounts is equally certain.

On September 2nd, the Exchange Rate was again altered to nine Reichsmarks to the pound sterling, while, to take the place, to some extent, of the vanishing silver, the States issued, in March 1941, the wholly insufficient quantity of £5,000 worth of locally printed two shilling *coupures*. A year later, after experiencing vast inconvenience and hardship, local currency notes of £1, 10s., 2s., 1s. and 6d. were printed ánd issued to take the place of British Treasury notes, but silver, no longer in circulation, was scarcely ever seen. At a later date, locally printed postage stamps of $2\frac{1}{2}d.$, $2d.$, $1\frac{1}{2}d.$, $1d.$ and

$\frac{1}{2}d$. came on sale at the local Post Office.

As time went on, with the exception of copper coinage, British currency completely disappeared. The greatly enhanced value of Treasury notes on the Continent, especially in terms of French francs, where at times the one pound note bore an equivalent value of as much as thirty-five shillings and over, led to their wholesale exportation by the Germans, who were not slow to take advantage of the situation. The Banks were helpless. They could not refuse to exchange Treasury notes for Reichsmarks at the Rate of Exchange of the day, since the latter were legal tender and current by order in the Island. I myself witnessed a transaction of the kind. A German officer presented himself at the Bank counter with a despatch-case full of Reichsmarks, and demanded, in Treasury notes, no less a sum than £800. He duly received it; but the face of the unhappy cashier, as he struggled with a vast mountain of dirty paper marks, I well remember, was a study.

Some time afterwards, the German Authorities, doubtless with a view to the eventual confiscation of any bearer bonds deposited by their owners for safe custody, insisted upon examining the contents of the Banks' strong rooms. This examination must have proved a bitter disappointment for, with great prudence and foresight, the respective managers had shipped the whole of the negotiable securities in their possession to England by the last mail steamer to leave. At a later date, however, the Germans took possession of the whole of the Bank of England and British Treasury notes in the hands of the banks. I have been informed that, with a view to rendering this money useless in such an eventuality, the managers of the Jersey banks had proposed to the States to mark the notes by perforation with some such words as 'For Circulation in Jersey only' or other formula to that effect. For the adoption of this simple remedy, the States, fearing a charge of sabotage, did not see their way to afford the necessary authority. As the result, I understand, the Banks lost between eighty and ninety thousand pounds. To make the decision of the Jersey Civil Authorities the more inexplicable and exasperating, at this time the Banks were taking in many thousands of pounds each week in German Reichsmarks, valueless elsewhere, which they were compelled to credit in sterling to customers depositing them.

CHAPTER TWO

EARLY DAYS OF THE OCCUPATION

ONE of the first objects to which the new-comers devoted their attention was the rapid impoverishment and destruction of Jersey's trade. To achieve this, they proceeded, with the aid of their paper Reichsmarks, finally given the fictitious value of two shillings and three halfpence each, to purchase and send out of the Island practically every article that such money would buy. Soon the shop windows of St. Helier began to present a depressingly empty appearance. All day long you might have seen German officers and men, burdened by packages and parcels, hurrying back to their billets. These men, I learned, provided with money especially for the purpose, entered business premises intent upon exhausting the goods on sale. Jewellery, gold and silverware, watches and clocks, men's and women's clothing, underclothing, furs, haberdashery, footwear, toilet articles and perfumery, fancy goods, nothing came amiss. Even uncut bolts of cloth from the tailors, household linen, blankets, sheets, curtains and curtain material, carpets and linoleum, all were feverishly bought up. Finally, when these classes of goods were exhausted, the insatiable buyers turned their attention to gas-fires, electrical apparatus, ironmongery, anything, in a word, that could be purchased, packed up and sent away.

It was not long, therefore, before shop windows, completely or almost completely bare, were boarded over, partly to safeguard their expensive and irreplaceable plate glass, but chiefly because, behind them, there was nothing left to display. Soon the larger and more commodious premises, Burton's, Woolworth's and the Fifty Shilling Tailors, were taken over and transformed into a Soldiers' Canteen, a Wine and Spirit

33

Depôt for seized or requisitioned wines and spirits, a Propaganda Centre for the diffusion of Nazi literature and the like. But large stocks of alcoholic liquor were centralised at other places. Champagne, brandy and other luxuries of the kind, unprocurable by the civilian population, were earmarked for the use of the German officers.

Very soon after the arrival of the German troops, dances were arranged by them in the two principal dance halls of St. Helier. No German festivity, or course, can possibly be a success unless accompanied by large supplies of German beer. Beer, therefore, in great quantities, was imported to ensure such a spirit as the Teutonic mind regards as festive. These dances were attended by all ranks, officers, non-commissioned officers and men, but after several of these gatherings had failed to attract a single female member of what might be called the *haute société* of the Island, great disgust was expressed by the officers, whose 'conquests' had perforce to be limited to domestic servants, the young damsels from behind the various lesser counters of the business world and—others. That many had cause, later, to regret the intimacies to which these dances led is a matter which will be dealt with hereafter. Towards the end of 1940, probably to mark the disappointment of the officers at their failure to attract the ladies of the Island to their balls and dances, indulgence in this form of amusement was suddenly prohibited.

A year or so later, a number of German theatricals and variety companies were brought over, as well as German films for the local cinemas, where, however, manifestations of applause or displeasure were sternly forbidden. At the same time, hordes of French prostitutes were imported, and lodged in hotels and empty private houses, which were thus readily transformed into convenient brothels for the use of German officers and others.

About this time, complete control of all ports and harbours was vested in a German Port Authority. This control applied also to every description of vessel, including fishing boats. No boat could proceed to fish without a licence. As a consequence, enthusiasm for fishing, not for many years very exuberant in

34

Jersey, received a further set-back. Moreover, as the Germans insisted on appropriating the greater part of each catch, the amount of fish left for the public was negligible.

The autumn of 1940 brought a shiver of apprehension to owners of the twelve thousand odd motor vehicles which, up to the arrival of the Germans, had circulated freely upon the roads of the Island. Teutonic cupidity being doubtlessly stirred by the spectacle of all these smart and, for the most part well-kept cars and lorries, a notice was inserted in the Press ordering registration with full particulars of all motor-cars, motor-cycles and other petrol-propelled vehicles. A few days later, an Order from the Field Commandant directed that private cars were to be presented at specified centres for valuation and purchase for the use of the German Army. Vehicles were examined and tested by persons appointed for the purpose in the presence of a German officer. In many cases, the cars were retained; in others, owners were directed to drive them home again, and to keep them in their possession until further notice. Cars in the latter category were said to be reserved, and document to that effect was affixed to their windscreens. In the settlement of prices, there appeared to be no sort of consistent rule; for while the owners of the smaller and less expensive types frequently received reasonable and often fairly high prices, great indignation was expressed at the valuation of higher-class vehicles.

In due time all the cars which had been reserved were called up and taken; the owners receiving, in place of cash, a curious document, issued by the States, in the nature of a bond. This interesting piece of paper informed the recipient that it entitled him to receive the amount stated therein *six months after the conclusion of the war!* The bond addressed to me entitling me to rather less than one-third of the value of a car which, with rage and bitterness I had handed over, I framed as a curio. For about two years it adorned the walls of my study until, one morning, to my profound surprise, I received an intimation that, on presenting it at the Treasury, the sum due to me stated thereon would be paid. And it was.

On the whole, I suppose I was lucky; for some there were

who, three years later, had received for their vehicles neither bonds nor cash.

Apparently with a view to impressing the phlegmatic Jersey public, troops parades were of frequent occurrence. The men were addressed with great force and vigour by the officer who had taken the salute. On one of these occasions, in September 1940, a certain General von Richthoven said, or rather strepitonated, that, as all must now be fully aware, the war had reached a stage whereat only one balance remained to be struck to bring a speedy and successful conclusion, the war with England. Never again, he solemnly assured his hearers, would there be a French War Machine; never again he vociferated, would there be a British Expeditionary Force.

Still further to depress the people of Jersey, on September 28th, 1940, the town was placarded, in lurid coluors, with a notice in English and German stating that one Marcel Brossier had been sentenced to death and shot for cutting a telephone cable.

Thenceforward, to the end of 1940, the islanders gradually and sensibly adapted themselves to new and unwelcome conditions. There was the daily spectacle of hordes of Germans wandering about the town of St. Helier, of troops bellowing marching songs at the top of their raucous voices; the punctilious salutes accorded by the men to officers and non-commissioned officers alike, the supercilious, high and mighty swagger of Corporal Hitler's officers as they disdainfully surveyed their new surroundings or regarded the unaccountable people who, to their indignant astonishment, scarcely glanced in their direction.

Most prominent among the Orders issued by German Headquarters as 1940 drew to its close was one which directed all British males, from 18 to 35 years of age, to register on a form provided. This form, among many other intimate particulars of birth and parentage, included information as to whether the person registering had served in the Allied Forces of the Crown.

About the same time, meetings of societies, unions and associations of all kinds, the display of flags and the wearing of

36

decorations or distinguishing emblems were strictly prohibited. Identity cards with photographs of the bearer were ordered, while, on the last day of the year, the people of Jersey, on pain of death, were forbidden to keep carrier pigeons. As though this was insufficient, a week later, the keeping of pigeons of any kind was rigorously interdicted.

And now, for some days, if you should have been passing through the Royal Square of St. Helier, you would have witnessed a revolting sight. For many years, as in Trafalgar Square and St. Paul's Cathedral precincts in London, numbers of pigeons strutted about the pavement. These birds, fed daily by kind-hearted persons, had become so tame that they would scarcely get out of your way. Now German soldiers with huge nets were capturing the unfortunate birds by the dozen. They were then crammed into sacks and taken away to be killed and served up at the tables of the German officers.

Shortly afterwards, we were informed, in the usual flamboyant way, that Louis Bernier, for releasing a carrier pigeon with a message for England, had been sentenced to death and shot.

It was about this time that the first measures against Jews were published by the Civil Commandant. They read as follows:

1. Persons of Jewish religion, or who have more than two Jewish grandparents, are deemed to be Jews.

2. Jews who have fled from occupied Zones may not return there.

3. Every Jew must present himself for registration with his family.

4. Every business conducted by a Jew is to be designated a 'Jewish Undertaking,' in English, French and German.

5. Heads of Jewish communities must furnish all necessary documentary evidence.

6. Contravention is punishable by imprisonment, fine and confiscation of goods.

A few weeks later the foregoing Order was supplemented by the following additional demands:

1. A declaration of all shares belonging to or pledged to Jews.

2. A statement of their beneficial interest in any business.

3. A statement of their sleeping interest in any such business.

4. Particulars of any real estate held, or interest therein.

5. All legal transactions by Jews whereby goods were disposed of after May 23rd, 1940, were declared null and void.

6. It was notified that an Administrator for Jewish undertakings would be appointed.

On May 31st, 1941, it was intimated that persons having three grandparents of Jewish blood or two grandparents married to Jews were deemed to be Jews. It was further notified that from May 20th of that year, Jews were forbidden to carry on any of eighteen specified activities of the most ordinary character; that Administrators would be appointed to administer holdings of Jews in limited liability companies, with instructions to make no advances out of income arising therefore except for absolute necessities. No compensation, it was stated, would be paid in respect thereof, or to Jewish employees whom it might be found necessary to dismiss.

On June 26th, 1942, curfew for Jews was fixed at 8 p.m. to 6 a.m. For other persons 10 p.m. to 6 a.m.

Jews in Jersey, corresponding to the foregoing definitions, were not numerous. There were, however, a certain number of tradesmen and others of Jewish race. They were, I believe, estimable persons as a whole, against whom I had certainly never heard a word of either disparagement or detraction. That the measures taken by the Germans must have borne heavily against them, there can be no shadow of doubt, and I feel sure that they were the objects of much sympathy from all right minded persons.

Finally all Jews found in Jersey were deported to Germany.

On March 31st, another notice was widely placarded, as well as published in the Press, informing the public that 'for supporting England in the war against Germany' (nature of support not stated) a young man named Francois Scornet had been shot.

Throughout the weary period of the German Occupation the Military Authorities appeared to be constantly seeking means of every description to depress, dishearten and cast down into the lowest depths of despondency the civil population of Jersey. This they did in a variety of ways. What effect upon a world-war the state of mind or sympathies of a handful of Jersey people could have it is difficult to imagine. In spite of that, every possible means was employed to render their cheerless lives if possible a shade more cheerless.

First of all came the Press. Jersey journalism is confined to two newspapers. *The Evening Post* published in English, and *Les Chroniques de Jersey* printed in French. The German Authorities placed both of these publications under their control. Officers with special knowledge of Press work, and of the two languages, were at once appointed to take over and assume responsibility for all matter printed, especially German war *communiqués*. They saw to it that the public was well informed that the Axis Powers were winning the war hands down! The number and tonnage of British and Allied vessels claimed to be sunk by U-boats accounted for more ships, both naval and commercial, than the Allies ever possessed. The air raids on London and other English cities (always with negligible loss to the German Air Force) were so appalling that it seemed miraculous to readers that any buildings could still exist. The Allied armies in the field never, by any chance, achieved the smallest success; at every point they were invariably and with wearisome iteration annihilated, repulsed or thrown back with tremendous losses in men, material and equipment, and all their plans frustrated. Outstanding, in my recollection, almost immediately after Hitler's attack upon Russia in June, 1942, were the screaming headlines appearing in the German-controlled *Evening Post* announcing:

'EIGHT RUSSIAN ARMIES ANNIHILATED.
THE ROADS TO LENINGRAD AND MOSCOW
NOW OPEN TO US.'

39

And so, for years, the German *communiqués* went on. In vain one asked oneself 'What earthly purpose do these German journalists and their superiors imagine they are serving by the publication of these transparent lies?' It was probably hoped, by these mendacious means, to reduce the islanders to desperation and despair, while vaunting the unconquerable might of the German fighting machine.

In addition to the Jersey *Evening Post*, the Germans brought out a newspaper called the *Insel Zeitung*, published in their own tongue. This doubtless contained similar statements of mythical successes all over Europe and North Africa, and was intended to buttress and maintain the morale of the troops. Frequently it contained crude illustrations, destined for consumption in Germany, which indicated the rapidity with which German kultur was spreading, and the wonderful ease with which Channel Islanders were becoming Germanised. One, at least, of these illustrations was obtained in the following way. In the course of a band concert given in the Royal Square and largely attended by children and young people, at a given moment, the bandmaster attracted the attention of his juvenile audience by calling out that he had a question to ask them. He then enquired, with an insinuating air, if they liked chocolate, requesting those who did to raise their right arms. There naturally arose a forest of eager arms. That was the moment at which the waiting photographer pressed the button. The following day the current number of the *Insel Zeitung* contained a picture showing young Jersey standing at the Nazi salute while, the caption stated, the band was playing the Horst Wessel Song, or some other patriotic air.

The war *communiqués* at length became so outrageous in their blatant and obvious falsity that few continued to read them, except with a view to ascertaining from the place-names which they contained where exactly the fighting was taking place.

With the passage of the years, and as news-print became scarcer, the Island Press grew smaller and smaller. From four pages, the *Evening Post* dwindled to two, and, finally to one, more or less lengthy periods occurring in which, to our great relief, there was no publication at all. By many it was purchased merely in order to keep abreast of the spate of orders and regulations at which, on its appearance, the uneasy islanders apprehensively glanced, wondering, as they did so, where the lightning would strike next, upon whom the next blow would fall.

It should be remembered that, as a matter of course, during the years of German control, we received no English newspapers at all. People living at home in England can form no conception of the misery of being deprived, over a long period of time, of their familiar organ of daily home and world intelligence; of their morning illustrated news-sheet, with its up-to-the-minute résumé of the happenings of the last twenty-four hours—to say nothing of the fascinating crossword puzzle and lighter features. Often and wistfully we pictured to ourselves the admirably clear-cut excellence of the illustrations, plainly and distinctly depicting every phase, every aspect of the titanic struggle of which we only occasionally caught dim and doubtful echoes. We could not but feel that what we were missing was a loss for which the future could never compensate us, and it never can.

By passing Allied aircraft, illustrated leaflets, printed in English and indicating the progress of the fighting, were occasionally dropped upon the Island. The first of these came while the islanders still remained in possession of their wireless sets, which had already amply confirmed their contents. But the news presented in the leaflets, some of which were of American origin, was at such complete variance with the falsehoods published in the German-controlled Island Press as to arouse the fury of the occupying Authority. No sooner, therefore, was it reported that a shower of these welcome intelligence sheets had fallen than squads of field-grey clad soldiers were despatched to gather them up, or at least all that they could find. With curious simple-minded *naïveté*, their officers forbade the men to read the retrieved leaflets, or even to glance at the illustrations which they contained. They could not have reflected that such an order would demand rather more of youthful curiosity than the men could afford. With similar

41

prohibitions, and under pain of terrible punishments including fine, imprisonment and even death for the offence of retaining, reading, or communicating them, civilians were ordered immediately to deliver up to the Authorities all copies of these intelligence sheets which might come into their possession. Almost needless to say, however, they were eagerly read and passed from hand to hand until they became so worn as to be almost illegible. But how good they were to read and gloat over! And how senders and pilots alike were blessed, for, in addition to the light-hearted letter-press, they contained amusing caricatures, much appreciated humorous sketches, and by their effervescent, high-spirited wit, served to bring into many a gloomy, care-stricken family a much needed ray of optimism. Stories were even told of small wireless receiving sets, attached to miniature parachutes, boxes of almost forgotten chocolates and cigarettes raining down from on high as planes passed over. Of these, however, I for one had no personal experience or knowledge, and those fortunate ones (if any) into whose grounds they fell, were as mysterious and unidentifiable as alleged beholders of the fabled Indian rope trick.

At a much later date, at a time, indeed, when, due to our rapid successes in Normandy and Brittany, the troops in occupation of Jersey were as much prisoners in the Island as the civil population had for so long been, other leaflets in German entitled *Nachrichten für die Truppe* were showered upon us. These, prepared by the Allies, contained, among other things, authentic and well-chosen reports of the German *débacle* in France and Belgium and had an effect upon German morale far greater that that produced by their official Press *communiqués*.

Late in the summer of 1940, a regulation was adopted by the States decreeing that household furniture and effects, abandoned in their houses by persons who had hastily quitted the Island, should be stored in the custody of a designated official, and in no case sold or otherwise disposed of until forty days after the return of the respective owners. It was time. By the early autumn, innumerable cases of burglarious entry into such premises were almost daily reported. Wholesale thefts engaged, day after day, the attention of the harassed Police. In a few cases arrests were made and the stolen property recovered, but, in the great majority, it was never seen again.

In the weeks that followed, some progress was made in giving effect to the States' directions, but, before more than a small fraction of the work could be completed, an Order from the German Commandant stopped all further progress. This Order prohibited the removal of furniture of any description from abandoned houses, such furniture being required, it was stated, at short notice, for the use of the Army of Occupation.

A few weeks later, Administrators of persons who had left for England were ordered, within five days, to present duplicate inventories of all furniture which had been stored belonging to such persons. Soon afterwards, all single mattresses left by evacuees were ordered to be handed over forthwith and for days afterwards, lorries piled high with this class of bedding, in all states of preservation, might have been seen proceeding in the direction of the indicated *dépôt*. It is perfectly safe to say that these, together with the whole of the furniture commandeered, were for ever lost to unfortunate owners. While it is highly improbable that any claim would ever be made for the return of the mattresses, after their use by German soldiers, the fate of the furniture, much of which was of considerable value, is less shrouded in mystery, for much of it was openly shipped to Germany. It was credibly stated that, during the later phases of the war, great quantities of household effects of all kinds, together with similar articles looted from French occupied towns and villages, were loaded, in neighbouring ports, into trains destined for German centres which had suffered from our bombing. These trains bore white painted notices stating that the contents of the wagons were spontaneously presented, by the sympathetic peoples of France and the English Channel Islands, to unfortunate German families, to atone, in some degree, for the barbarous and inhuman destruction wrought upon innocent and defenceless German civilians by murderous Allied aircraft.

Among the largest and most important buildings in Jersey are the Maison Saint Louis, Highland College, and the Jersey

College for Girls. Each stands in its own beautiful and extensive grounds and occupies a commanding position overlooking the town. All three are very large and extremely handsome. The Maison Saint Louis is a Jesuit seminary for the training of young Frenchmen for the priesthood; it probably provided accommodation and instruction for about one hundred and fifty students. The others, also important educational establishments, afforded residential and educational advantages for large numbers of young people.

Soon all three buildings were requisitioned for the German Army of Occupation. The first named, its students hurriedly shipped off to France, was transformed into barracks for the troops; Highland College being utilised for the same purpose. For the Jersey College for Girls, a particularly hideous fate was reserved. The fine and tastefully decorated class-rooms and dormitories were devoted to the reception of a horde of Russian prisoner-labourers, men who were forced to exist in an habitual condition of dirt so unspeakably dreadful that the quarters in which they were herded speedily became foul and verminous. When these men were later sent away, the building was utilised as a hospital for wounded troops and marines from the French coast ports.

The condition in which these fine buildings were left was indescribable, and sheds a further ray of light on, and adds to one appreciation of, the thing called German kultur.

But the larger and more important houses taken over as quarters for German officers, even where furniture and appointment were not exported, were despoiled. Thus, senior officers residing in one house, taking a fancy to pictures, carpets or other objects of value seen in premises occupied by men of junior rank, would unhesitatingly order such objects to be sent to them for their use. In this way, the original owners, returning to Jersey at the end of the war, may spend months, perhaps years, in tracing, recognising and reclaiming their property discovered, it may be, miles away in the involuntary possession of persons possibly unknown to them.

Empty houses were treated in a shocking manner. In many, dividing walls between rooms were roughly broken through;

staircases were torn down for firewood; water-closets were choked up and, where this happened, cellars and basements were used as lavatories until the premises became untenable, when they were evacuated and other dwellings occupied with similar results. In one private house at St. Brelade's the drawing-room afforded accommodation for a number of pigs. It may be said that, in many cases, houses tenanted by German troops were left in such a sorry condition that they were only fit to be pulled down and re-erected.

In addition to houses vacated by their owners or occupants on their departure from the Island, any dwelling house in town or country which appeared to be convenient or desirable for some alleged military purpose, or as temporary quarters for officers or men, was promptly requisitioned; the owner or tenant in actual occupation receiving a curt notice to quit and find accommodation for himself and his family elsewhere. Often the unfortunate householder was given but two or three days in which to do so, and had the greatest difficulty in securing another roof to cover him. Scarcely a dwelling in the Island was safe. One never knew the day or hour when one might be summarily dispossessed, and one's belongings, or such of them as were not required by the incoming Germans, thrust into the roadway. Here was another grinding anxiety added to life, an anxiety from which, until the invasion of Normandy by our troops, one was never free. Scores upon scores of people suffered in this way; I myself only escaping through a purely fortuitous circumstance.

A military zone, which included all coasts and coastal roads, was declared in May 1941. Persons residing, or having business therein were compelled to provide themselves with special passes. Curfew, moreover, was fixed one hour earlier than elsewhere in these areas. The general idea underlying this Order was to keep the public away from works connected with island fortification which were now proceeding apace. At the same time, the sea beaches, as well as the land behind them, were heavily mined. Dogs seen trespassing in the forbidden zone were ordered to be shot.

Later in the year, the inhabitants of Jersey were ordered, for billeting purposes, to deliver to a specified authority, schedules showing the number of bedrooms and other rooms in their houses, the number of persons habitually sleeping there, and full particulars regarding lighting, cooking, water supply and drainage. At a later date, in a number of cases, German officers and soldiers were compulsorily billeted in private houses. In many instances, I was informed, these men were inoffensive and gave little trouble; but in others, especially where the family included girls and young women, the conduct of the Germans, at times, was odious. Any attempt to restrain them by force was the immediate signal for the drawing of a revolver or a bayonet, and was almost certain to be followed by some trumped-up charge which consigned the unhappy parent, husband, or brother to a more or less lengthy term of imprisonment during which, of course, the house and its remaining inmates were left without protection.

The Spring of 1941 witnessed the first of a number of epidemics of burglary which, during the German Occupation of Jersey, broke out in the Island. In addition to thefts from evacuated houses to which reference has already been made, tradesmen's shops, with great regularity and frequency, were the scenes of these nocturnal visits, the time usually selected being the eve of the issue of rationed foodstuffs, tobacco and cigarettes. In many cases, these goods were swept away in such quantities as to arouse suspicion that there was already a steady Black Market growing up for their disposal. In the month of May the first of several very extensive thefts from the Food Control Store was reported, and about the same time, the abstraction, from the Jersey Mental Hospital, of a very large quantity of tea (already unobtainable in the Island) gave rise to much suggestive criticism.

By this time the German Authorities had begun the importation of a number of police officials who were billeted in the various hotels. They were not, apparently, at first connected with the notorious Gestapo, but appeared to fulfil the functions of spies upon the civil population, making themselves at times, by their harsh, brutal churlishness, one more terror added to life. These men would violently force their way where wireless (at that time officially permitted) was being listened to, and, characterising the *communiqué* in course of broadcast as 'lies, lies,' would brusquely order it to be turned off. They would impudently intrude into private conversations, demanding the meaning of some overheard remark made or expression used. On one occasion, at a well-known hotel, one of these blackguards, observing that an old lady present was wearing a brooch in the form of the well-known badge of the Royal Air Force which had been given to her by her son, scowlingly and peremptorily ordered her to remove it. This she very naturally refused to do. The German then ordered her husband, a retired Indian judge, to be summoned. On the latter's arrival, the demand was still more offensively repeated, the police officer expressing his intention, if this order were not obeyed, to tear the brooch off the lady's dress. The indignant husband, unfortunately losing his temper, threatened that, if this was done, he would knock the policeman down, whereupon the German, drawing his revolver, called in a subordinate and, violently taking possession of the brooch complained of, arrested the furious judge who was immediately removed on a charge of resisting police authority. He was sentenced to a lengthy term of imprisonment on the Continent. Distraught with grief, his wife took to her bed and died. This incident and its pathetic sequel aroused great and widespread indignation.

But spying on the civil population continued and, as time went on, became almost a commonplace. It took a variety of forms.

After the final confiscation of wireless receiving sets, every effort was made by the German authorities not only to discover persons who had had the courage to retain them, but also those who communicated wireless intelligence to their friends and neighbours. These latter were often pleasantly accosted in the street by well dressed persons speaking perfect English. They would be asked in cheery tones if they had had any news that day from one or other of the fighting fronts, whether or not it was a fact that such and such a city had been taken by the Allies, or again, after lamenting the increasing scarcity of

47

some commodity, whether it was still obtainable in England. If a definitely informative reply was elicited, the individual approached would be asked how he came by his knowledge, and, in all probability, he would promptly find himself undergoing a gruelling examination, with disastrous results, before the officials of the Gestapo.

Spies, frequently females, would stand in the milk queues with their jugs, and listen to gossip. Conversations in omnibuses, in particular, and in the streets were also liable to be overheard by the ubiquitous German spies. You could not safely refer in any way to the war or to war intelligence outside the security of your own home, and not even there if you were unwise enough to employ servants of Continental nationality.

Some misguided individuals there were who would foolishly carry on their persons written transcripts of the wireless *communiqués*. These, on discovery, or on denunciation by persons with a grudge (which occasionally happened), were dealt with most severely.

Throughout the years of the German Occupation of the Channel Islands, the occupying Authorities, in Jersey at any rate, received large numbers of anonymous letters from local people denouncing fellow islanders and others for possessing hidden wireless receiving sets. These precious missives, conceived in a spirit of the most contemptible spite, frequently resulted in most serious consequences to persons accused, whose houses were promptly and thoroughly rummaged and searched from basement to attic. There can be little doubt that spies were tempted by the rewards for denunciations which the German Authorities are said to have offered, and it was not unknown, it must be regrettably admitted, for one member of a family to denounce another.

In March 1942, all British subjects of United Kingdom birth were forbidden to dispose of locally-situated landed property, securities, shares, money values, debts, copyright or patents. They were further ordered to send four copies of a full and accurate declaration respecting them to the Civil Commandant. This Order cannot have been very widely complied with, for many of the proprietors of landed property had left the Island, while securities of all kinds, especially 'bearer' securities, had, as I have stated elsewhere, been thoughtfully sent to London by the banks. Still, this was a disquieting indication which seemed to indicate in which way the wind was blowing. To all appearance, however, the absence of property owners and the difficulties attendant upon the identification and appropriation of their belongings must have outweighed any advantage to be derived from taking over and disposing of them, but British born subjects who complied with the direction must have passed many anxious days and nights before it became apparent that no action in the matter was to be taken.

On July 1st, 1941, it was reported that, two nights before, Colonel Britton's celebrated V-sign had been painted, doubtless by high-spirited young people, on certain houses and road surfaces in the St. Helier and St. Saviour's parishes. To these V-signs the German Authorities, having received an explanation of their significance from some obliging person, took the strongest objection. Therefore, an official Notice over the signature of the Attorney General, appeared in the Press. This Notice announced that the painting of the V-sign as described constituted an act of sabotage, and that dwellers in districts specified were ordering to furnish nightguards for the prevention of the recurrence of the offence; that all radio sets in the parishes named would be confiscated; and that a fine (amount not stated) would be levied on each parish. This notice aroused much unfavourable comment.

On July 28th, three persons found guilty of painting V-signs were sentenced to one year and two to nine months imprisonment by the German Military Court. On October 25th, however, V-signs were again discovered in three places in St. Helier.

It was not long after this, however, before the Germans themselves made use of the V-sign which was seen daily, surrounded by an artistic laurel-wreath, painted upon the wings of officers' motor-cars.

Scarcely had the annoyance aroused by the V-sign incidents died away than it was discovered that a telephone-line in use by the troops had been cut or broken. Immediately sabotage was charged upon the civil population. Without any attempt at enquiry the arrest of ten persons residing in the neighbourhood was ordered. These unfortunates, it was explained, would be held as hostages, and a further intimation stated that unless the perpetrator of the alleged sabotage was discovered, they would be sent to Germany for internment. A warning was added that any repetition of the offence would be followed by the arrest and deportation of twenty persons residing nearest to the act complained of. Whether these high-handed proceedings were actually carried into effect I was unable to ascertain; but I learned that the ten persons originally arrested were committed to prison whence, in all probability, they were sent to Germany.

A few days later all cameras and photographic apparatus of every description were ordered to be surrendered under penalty of fine or imprisonment. This was a particularly gratuitous demand since no sensitised films or plates for photographic work were anywhere longer obtainable. As the result, hundreds of cameras, many of the most modern and expensive types, were arbitrarily taken from their powerless possessors who, of course, never saw them again until after the liberation.

But, whenever the events of 1942 are recalled, the year's outstanding atrocity, and one which for sheer calculated inhumanity transcends any other inflicted upon an inoffensive peaceable section of the island population, is brought to mind. By an Order from the Military Commandant, dated September 15th, British subjects born in the United Kingdom, between the ages of 16 and 70, residing in the Island of Jersey at the date of the Occupation, together with their families, were ordered to be transferred to Germany to be there interned. It will be observed that the order dealt remorselessly with British subjects born in the United Kingdom; those from the Irish Free State, being theoretically neutrals, together with those from the British Dominions and Colonies, as also those of Jersey birth, were not included.

It will also be observed that the Order was in direct contravention of the solemn undertaking contained in the ultimatum of July 1st, 1940, which stated: 'In case of peaceful surrender (of the Island), the lives, property and liberty of peaceful inhabitants are solemnly guaranteed.'

In spite of that undertaking, some twelve hundred of His Majesty's subjects, men, women and children, of all ages within the limits stated, were immediately registered for evacuation, the first result being the sudden death, from shock and suicide, of not a few.

The week allowed for preparation and for such arrangements relating to the safeguarding of homes and property as could be made, must have been the darkest and bitterest which those unfortunate people had ever experienced. Many among them had lived in Jersey for years; the Island had become home to them in the fullest and most sacred significance of the word. Their houses and gardens and land, upon which they had lavished care and thought and money; their cherished household goods and effects, furniture, pictures, silver, often of considerable value and irreplaceable for its associations; their personal belongings and clothing; their many friends, powerless to help them now; all these must be suddenly abandoned and left behind in an island in enemy occupation. One can well imagine their hopelessness, their despair, the miserable realisation of the inexorcisable fact that, for no fault committed, they must quit their homes where many had hoped peacefully to live and die, and, with their wives and families, leave all they possessed at the mercy of men who knew no mercy. One's heart went out to those hapless people as, in the all too few days grudgingly allowed them, they looked their last upon all in this world that they valued and prized.

Their departure was a heart-rendering sight.

The streets of St. Helier leading to the port were closed to traffic and barred off by German troops, but, as the time of embarkation drew near and the deportees marched down towards the steamers, the men laden with the family's slender baggage, the women leading or carrying their wondering children, they presented an appearance of dignified, unruffled calm. Crowds had assembled to cheer them on their way, to offer a word of unneeded encouragement. And how those crowds cheered and waved hats and handkerchiefs! The general appearance of the occasion was rather that of a triumphant departure than of an exodus forced by the stony-hearted dictum of a pitiless, all-powerful enemy. They marched with heads erect, a smile of grateful recognition for friends in the throng. I went away with an unaccustomed constriction in my throat, but also burning with indignation and disgust. I could not but feel most deeply that those men and women of ours were indeed a credit to us all.

Conditions on the voyage to the French coast can only be described as appalling. Persons of culture and refinement accustomed to the comforts and amenities of well ordered homes, were violently thrust, by armed soldiers, into the foetid, bilge-smelling holds of small cargo steamers. They had no bedding, no light, no water, and there were no sanitary arrangements whatsoever.

A few months later a further deportation of British subjects to Germany took place. While their number was considerable, this later evacuation was on a smaller scale than that which had preceded it.

The fate of the deportees, both on the journey, which occupied six or seven comfortless days, and on arrival in the camps provided for their occupation, was unenviable in the extreme. As news gradually filtered back from them it appeared that, on reaching their respective destinations, they had suffered severely for some time from cold and hunger. There were many difficulties in the way of personal cleanliness and sanitation; there was, moreover, a complete absence of privacy. At night, the sexes were divided, thirty or forty persons in a building sleeping on straw mattresses with insufficient covering. All the work of the camp and its hutments, including the cooking of food, the scrubbing and cleansing of the floors, the making of beds, such as they were, and, indeed, everything else, was performed by the inmates.

Gradually system was evolved, and everybody was entrusted with a share of the welfare of the small communities. But it is not difficult to imagine the hardships, the squalor, for example, of the long monotonous days, the sleepless misery of the interminable nights.

After some little time, due to the kindly ministrations of the International Red Cross, the lot of the Jersey internees improved. They were supplied with additional foods and clothing, both of which were greatly needed. Books and other forms of literature were also received by them, and classes for the young people were formed in order that, in so far as might be possible, their education should not suffer complete interruption. At the same time, other classes for older persons wishing to study languages or to take elementary courses in engineering and natural science, were formed. By these and similar means, much time, which otherwise would have hung heavily upon their hands, was more pleasantly and profitably spent.

But their thoughts must often have turned to the homes left behind in Jersey, and wistfully enough they must have speculated upon what had happened or was happening to them. In many cases, it was, perhaps, just as well that they did not know.

In some instances, no doubt, where it had been possible to find friends able and willing to occupy vacated premises, little loss or damage resulted; but in others, in the great majority of cases, dwellings were left completely unoccupied, and they fell an easy prey to the burglars, who did untold damage.

In the years to come, however much of Jersey's sufferings during the German Occupation may fade from people's memory, the fate of the Island's deported residents will never be forgotten.

CHAPTER THREE

THE JACKBOOT

SINCE the so-called purchase of private motor-cars, already described, the bicycle in Jersey had come into its own. It was, of course, the only remaining means of moderately speedy transport.

Prices of bicycles soared. Disreputable, rusty old crocks for which their owners would gladly have accepted a few shillings six months before were now eagerly snapped up at anything up to ten pounds. Machines with any pretension to smartness or modernity changed hands at three and four times that sum. An order to present all bicycles for purchase by the Germans came, therefore, as a sharp blow, particularly since the Germans were not prepared to pay more for these enforced purchases than the valuers' estimated value which completely ignored the inflated prices created by the sudden demand.

Omnibuses too, were taken off the roads to an extent that became the despair of those living in the north of the island and elsewhere in the country districts. Transport became very difficult.

The adoption of improvised methods of transport became imperative. To provide these, large numbers of horses and horse-drawn vehicles of all kinds were brought over from the Continent, and soon these animals and the wagons, drays, carts, carriages and other conveyances which they drew were daily seen in constantly increasing numbers. Splendid draught horses were imported and, in the last years of the Occupation, undoubtedly fulfilled a most useful purpose.

In certain conditions, farmers who had been deprived of their petrol lorries were permitted the use of these horses, and were thus enabled to solve the very difficult and pressing problem of the transport of their various crops to the markets and elsewhere. Finally, from the end of 1944 onward, many of these fine animals were slaughtered to provide meat for the troops.

Shortly before the events last recorded, the rule of the road had been changed from the left side to the right. Great confusion and many accidents were anticipated, but the new system came into use smoothly and without incident or inconvenience. After a reasonable trial, it was felt that the change had much to recommend it, for foot-passengers, who usually instinctively kept to the right, found themselves facing oncoming traffic, and lost all desire to step off the pavement into the roadway. A return to the original system, has, however, since been made.

Reference has already been made to the curious vacillating, cat-and-mouse character of the German procedure regarding wireless receiving sets. This appeared to be the move incomprehensible since, from the first day of their presence in the Island, with steeled hearts, the public had felt convinced that they would be compelled to give them up. Some surprise, not unmingled with relief, had been felt when the first Order issued actually left them in our hands, even at the cost of being compelled to listen only to German and German-controlled stations. We felt that, in any case, we retained them, and that, in itself, was an unhoped-for mercy.

Such being the case, our joy may not be imagined when a fortnight after the Order referred to, we were informed that, 'in recognition of good behaviour,' we were to be permitted to listen in to any station. Life, we felt, was not, after all, wholly unbearable since, once more, we could hear London calling, the booming of Big Ben, and news upon which we could thoroughly rely. Our exultation, however, was premature; soon, all too soon, we were again destined to be stricken.

On October 17th, 1940, by decree of the Field Commandant, all wireless receiving sets were ordered to be given up. We gritted our teeth and began the task of preparing them for surrender. There then came an anxious pause during which hope waxed and waned as day followed day without definite instructions.

Came November 12th, and with it despair, when the Press published a curt intimation to the effect that all wireless receiving sets, the property of the civil population of Jersey, were to be confiscated. Upon this, hope died within us.

On the 28th of the same month, to our complete bewilderment, the last quoted Order was revoked, conditionally upon continued good behaviour.

Life thereupon renewed its relative normal aspect. Once again we set our machines in their accustomed places. Once again Big Ben, to say nothing of the well remembered Greenwich 'pips', enabled us to correct our time. These happy conditions continued again until a cloud appeared upon the horizon. This time it took the form of an Order from the States dated July 5th, 1941, which directed that, under penalty of a fine of five hundred pounds or two years imprisonment, all all-mains wireless receiving sets, the property of persons who had left the Island, should be given up by the 9th—four days only! Why the *ukase* exclusively specified all-mains sets was never made clear; neither were the public informed of the ultimate fate of the sets penalised.

For a full year thereafter we remained in undisturbed reception of our daily wireless news and entertainment. It had become once more a valued if scarcely considered item of the day's experiences when, on June 6th, 1942, came the final Order. On that date, all wireless receiving sets, except those in possession of the Germans, were ordered to be confiscated under penalty of a fine of 30,000 Reichsmarks (£3,000) and six months imprisonment. It was the end. Once more, and quite needlessly, we swathed the shining cases in whatever we possessed to protect them from injury, for we never saw them again. With rage in our hearts we handed them over to the tender mercies of those to whose custody they were ordered to be confided.

Some of us endeavoured to extract a grain of comfort and hope from an assurance, officially printed on June 12th, which stated that the confiscation was for military purposes only;

that the sets would be kept in safe custody, and that they would be returned to their owners when reasons for their withdrawal ceased to exist. But this was never done. Many were coolly appropriated by the troops, many more were openly exported to the Continent, one entire sling-load, in course of shipment, going overboard into the harbour.

In a few instances, from natives of the Irish Free State who were regarded as neutrals, sets were purchased by the Germans and fair prices paid; but in the great majority of cases owners received nothing. Still, we could not but feel that the confiscation of our wireless receiving sets could mean one thing and one thing only, namely, that events in Europe were going pretty badly for the enemy, and there was consolation in that.

But all the sets were not given up. There were in our midst a number of courageous people, and may their names be honoured for it, who, braving the heavy penalties threatened, managed to secrete their machines and soon, with infinite precaution, summaries of the day's war *communiqués* were whispered abroad or passed from hand to hand in matchboxes, cigarette-paper cartons, and other things. We were thus, for the most part, kept *au courant* of what was passing in the various theatres of the conflict, and the depressing effect of the Ananias-produced news published in the German controlled local Press was largely neutralised.

The searching of houses suspected of concealing wireless sets was brutal. Without notice, the Gestapo would descend upon your dwelling, at any hour of the day or night, and with complete thoroughness ransack it for the prohibited sets from cellar to attic. No piece of furniture escaped examination. The cushions of easy chairs, the bedding, even the floorboards, wainscoting and panelling were keenly scrutinised, and in the end you were left, without a word of regret or apology, to put your disordered things away again.

Numberless were the hair-breadth escapes. One woman, advised less than a minute before the arrival of the unwelcome visitors, evaded them by covering her small set with a large tea-cosy and carrying it out in her hands as they began their search. Another was compelled to destroy her apparatus by plunging it into a large vessel full of soap-suds, which contained the week's washing. Many were the close shaves; but many, alas, were the unfortunates who paid in the end heavy and merciless penalties.

Soon the almost complete evasion of their carefully thought-out plans to keep the people in ignorance reached the ears of the German Authorities. Thenceforward, until the end of the Occupation, the prisons were crowded to suffocation with persons, many of position and respectability, found guilty either of possessing wireless receiving sets or furtively disseminating wireless intelligence. For these so-called offences the most vindictive penalties were imposed. Not only were offenders imprisoned locally, some were sent to serve their sentences in Continental places of confinement where their privations and sufferings were almost unendurable.

Towards the end of the Occupation, as hidden sets grew fewer in number, local ingenuity replaced them by the secret manufacture of perfectly efficient hand-made sets. These, of primitive appearance, were remarkably cheap and highly satisfactory, and, in spite of their home-made appearance, reflected great credit on the skill and ingenuity of the makers. It was largely thanks to these comparatively rude contrivances that the progress of the Allied armies, during and after the invasion of Normandy, was followed by hundreds of Jersey people with complete confidence and, needless to say, breathless interest. These locally-made sets continued to keep the public informed until January 25th, when, due to the loss of our electric light, current was no longer available. Thereafter, crystal sets were improvised with surprisingly satisfactory results.

About a week after the Normandy Invasion, the houses of a number of retired British officers were entered in the middle of the night by the Germans. These officers were ordered to dress and proceed under escort to various destinations. On arrival, they were subjected to a certain amount of desultory questioning and, that concluded, were coolly told that they might return to their homes. One of these gentlemen informed me that his examination was of the most puerile description, and conveyed the impression that his questioner had little or no idea of what questions to ask, and, of so little importance were they, he made no notes of the answers he received. In the case of another, the intruders entered the officer's bedroom and stood there while he dressed, refusing to allow him even to go to the lavatory. No explanation of this outrageous conduct was vouchsafed either then or afterwards, but in the case of one, a Lieutenant-Colonel, on his complaining, an apology was received by him for the breach of military etiquette in sending a non-commissioned officer to summon him instead of an officer of equal rank.

This apparently gratuitous piece of purposeless annoyance, inflicted upon a number of perfectly innocuous men, is clear evidence of the condition of dithering, nervous obfuscation to which the invasion of Normandy, but thirty miles away, had reduced the German Command in the Channel Islands. Thenceforward, for many weeks, the civil population experienced great inconvenience from what, on the part of the Germans, can only be described as jitters. Not a doubt assailed the minds of commanding officers that the Island of Jersey would soon come under Allied attack. Vigilance was redoubled. Day and night manoeuvres were incessant. Tons of ammunition were discharged in gunnery, machine-gunnery, anti-aircraft gunnery and musketry practice. You would be sitting peaceably in your home at about 11 o'clock at night, when approaching rifle fire, volleys of blank cartridges coming nearer and nearer, would divert your attention exasperatingly from your book or card game. Soon discharges from under your windows would deafen you as troops, blazing away at nothing and even without bringing their rifles to the Present, tramped with jest and laughter, over your lawns and flower-beds, breaking down your shrubs and bushes, and creating the general havoc which greeted your indignant gaze the following morning. If you should have ripening fruit on your trees, the morning would show you with what complete thoroughness, in a surprisingly short space of time, the bulk of it could disappear. There was, of course, no redress; military necessity would at once have been hurled at you had you been unwise enough to utter a word of complaint.

Immediately upon intelligence of the invasion of Normandy reaching Jersey, small forces known as Alarm Squads were detached from Company Headquarters and moved to strategic points all over the Island. Wherever a stretch of open road presented a field of fire, gangs of men, fatigue parties in a word, armed with spades and pick-axes, entered private gardens and proceeded to dig trenches and rifle pits. If you were lucky, these were small—no larger in fact than was necessary to accommodate a single sniper; but in many cases where gardens were large, lengthy trenches, both straight and zig-zag, as well as deep bomb-shelters capable of affording refuge to a number of men, were excavated to a depth of six or eight feet.

In my own case, I was called upon to provide sleeping room in my garage for about a dozen men under a non-commissioned officer, while in my gardens and grounds no less than seven trenches and shelters of various sizes were dug, some to a very considerable depth indeed. My gardens also were utilised for the concealment of a large 3-inch howitzer, and an anti-tank gun, entrances and exits of which cut up my drive in a remarkably efficient manner. In my meadow beyond, an immense army lorry was concealed by digging out a space large enough to contain it in the sides of a descending bank, and covering it with branches torn from my bushes and trees. During the six or eight weeks of this occupation of my premises, we were never free from these youthful warriors, who treated my property exactly as if it had been their own, borrowed all sorts of things from the kitchen, and tried to make friends with our maids. Apart from that, however, I must record in all fairness that they did their best to give us as little trouble as possible, were perfectly polite, and were most appreciative and grateful for any slight help which they received from us.

Gradually the panic fear of invasion subsided, the Alarm Squads were withdrawn from this agreeable picnic existence, and, to their great discontent, were returned, to our relief to their respective Company Headquarters.

I have written elsewhere in this book of the great spread of theft and burglary which, from the beginning of the German Occupation, swept over the Island. I do not think that at its onset at any rate, it could be more than very slightly attributable to German agency; there were other elements much more likely to have become engaged in crime of this description.

But, soon after the establishment in Jersey of the Army of Occupation, for the many works of fortification which it saw fit to undertake, a large number of Russians were imported into the Island. These wretched creatures, many of whom were convicts liberated during the German advance into their country, others being prisoners of war, were housed in camps specially provided for them. These camps were theoretically guarded at night, but in so negligent and perfunctory a manner that, throughout the years 1942 and 1943, the prisoners often escaped either singly or in small bands. Once free, almost mad with hunger, for their rations were admittedly quite insufficient, especially in view of the hardness of the daily toil which fell to their lot, they set out in all directions intent upon plundering farms and dwelling houses. After a time, encouraged by their success, their raids increased not only in frequency but in the numbers who took part in them. Nothing was safe; cattle, pigs, fowls, potatoes, corn, vegetables, all these and much more were nightly stolen. Daylight theft of clothing from clothes-lines and out-houses, was common. If complaint were made, the stereotyped reply was: 'Well, they are your allies. Do you expect us to protect you from them?' In only one case did I hear of active intervention; a countrywoman living in close proximity to a large camp complained to the officer in charge of the theft of her entire week's 'wash'. On receiving some such reply as that quoted above, she remarked composedly that the theft did not really matter to her as the articles stolen were the property of Germans for whom she was acting as a temporary laundress. The weather then completely changed. With great promptitude and excitement the Camp Commandant rushed about ordering the institution of a thorough search, in the course of which the whole of the missing articles were speedily recovered.

Encouraged by almost complete immunity, Russian thieves

soon became dangerous. Country folk, farmers and others, disturbed in the middle of the night by the sound of prowlers and sallying forth to investigate, were frequently attacked. In one case, an unfortunate farmer was actually killed while attempting to defend his property.

In March 1943, during an attempted raid by four Russians upon a farm at St. Ouen, when attacked the farmer put up so good a fight that two of the marauders were killed and one severely injured. To make matters worse, it was stated that these Russians were repeatedly found to be acting under the orders of their guards who accompanied them on their forays, stood by while they carried them out, and, needless to say, appropriated the more attractive portion of the loot.

During the early part of 1944, most of the Russian labourers were withdrawn from Jersey, and although robberies by night continued, matters improved.

The unfortunate Russian prisoners were, I am convinced, driven to the crimes which they undoubtedly committed in Jersey by the frightful brutality which they received from their guards. The latter wore a distinctive military uniform, and, as a whole, were men of a low, cruel type, specially selected for their work. Ruthless, they treated their charges with pitiless inhumanity. These ruffians not only connived at the crimes committed, but are known to have ordered out their prisoners and to have shown them eligible premises to plunder.

Late in the month of August 1944, the fall of St. Malo brought to Jersey many German naval ratings and other refugees from that port who had unfortunately succeeded in evading the vigilance of our Naval Forces on the French coast. This, for Jersey people, already feeling the acute stringency of the food situation, was nothing short of a calamity, since the arrival of these large bodies of men meant so many additional mouths to feed. Their needs, I was informed, finally became so heavy that an all round reduction in military rations became imperatively necessary, notwithstanding the fact that, to make some sort of provision for the sailors, demands for large additional requisitions of cereals and potatoes, to the obvious detriment of the public, were received by the Civil Authorities.

Soon a positive feud sprang up between the troops already in occupation and the naval newcomers, the former accusing the latter of coming to eat them out of house and home instead of surrendering to the Allies as they might very properly have done. From words they speedily came to blows. Fights and disturbances were frequent and not easily quelled, for the men of the navy appeared to be far less amenable to discipline than their military brethren. To such a pitch, indeed, did their violent distaste for the soldiers reach that, at one time, over a considerable period, they refused to salute military officers.

In order to supplement their rations, of which they bitterly complained, these men of the sea speedily turned their attention to theft from the civil population. There can be no doubt that, with the waning of the year, marauding forays on farms and country houses, equalling those carried out by the Russians, increased once more in frequency.

The Civil Police were powerless, being unarmed and forbidden, in cases of infractions of the law by Germans, to effect arrests or to do more than summon the forces of the Field Gendarmerie who, being summoned, were almost always unable or unwilling to cope with the malefactors.

On the night of February 20th, 1945, the naval men turned out in great numbers, led, it was said, by some of their officers. Throughout the hours of darkness they must have worked with an energy worthy of a better cause for, when daylight came, the fronts of public buildings, business premises, shops and private houses were found to have been disfigured by the addition to their walls of Nazi swastikas, many five and six feet in height, daubed with coal tar wherever a flat surface presented itself. This was proved by many eye-witnesses to have been the work of the naval men, provided with ladders and large pots of tar, who moved swiftly in motor-cars from point to point defacing every building they passed in all parts of the town.

The indignation and disgust of the townspeople may easily

be imagined. Tar on plaster and cement cannot be erased except by destroying the surface to which it is applied. For many weeks, therefore, this wanton outrage continued to remind the good people of St. Helier of a debt to the naval detail of the troops in occupation which they would have been very eager to pay—in their own way.

Complaints to the German Authorities by officials of the States (for, on this occasion, I have been assured, representations were actually made) obtained little satisfaction. The Germans first attempted to accuse the large Irish colony in the Island of the offence complained of, but when irrefutable proof of the identity of the culprits was adduced, the Jersey officials, on suggesting that those guilty of the defacement should be ordered in so far as it might be possible to remove it, were coolly told that such a proposal could not be considered, as the ridicule to which the sailors would assuredly be subjected whilst engaged upon the task would be likely to provoke regrettable incidents.

For some time speculation was rife as to the reasons for the perpetration of this exasperating act of childish vandalism. I have been credibly assured that what lay at the bottom of the matter was a feeling of jealous rage against the civil population who, the sailors had been told, were in constant receipt, through the International Red Cross, of luxurious food parcels, while the troops in occupation were subsisting painfully, at the point of starvation, upon inadequate rations, meagrely supplemented by the flesh of horses, raw turnips and whatever else they were able to loot from the farms and gardens of the Island.

As 1944 drew to its close the attitude of the German Authorities, especially towards the farming industry, became increasingly oppressive. They proceeded to search farms for such commodities as unmilled wheat and potatoes, under the impression that the farmer, taking advantage of a satisfactory harvest, had secreted for his own use large quantities of these commodities. Some probably had, for, in previous years, growers had been specifically authorised to retain for themselves and their families certain percentages of their wheat and potato harvests. In 1944, however, I understand that this privilege had been withdrawn, as it was considered that, in the interests of the public—and the Germans—the entire yields should be handed, less a certain microscopical quantity saved from threshing, to the Department of Essential Commodities or Agriculture. This, to my mind at least, was a particularly inconsiderate act of unsympathetic treatment to extend to a hard-working and indispensable section of the community. If, therefore, the farming industry did in fact take reasonable measures from the means within its grasp to secure itself against hunger, I can only say small blame to it.

Although there were farmers who, while refusing to sell their produce to their fellow islanders, are known to have disposed of it at inflated prices to the Germans, this inexcusable conduct was not universal. To their credit, there were others who, throughout the Occupation, set their faces against this practice and refused at any time to have dealings with enemy troops.

But the reduction in military rations, to which I have already referred, was a further catastrophe for the farmers. Widespread nocturnal theft, committed not only by individuals but by bands of military and naval thieves, grew even worse.

September in Jersey is a month during which, although cereals have naturally been already harvested, potatoes and other root crops are still in the ground and apples and pears are on the trees. In the Island, in addition to a civil population of close upon 39,000, we had upwards of 10,000 hungry young Germans, many of whom were scarcely more than boys. Temptation was difficult to resist.

That these depredations were the work of bands of soldiers and sailors is evidence from the fact that, in one night and from one farm, several hundredweight of potatoes were carried away, leaving the unfortunate farmer with scarcely enough for his family's needs. In another case, nearly four hundredweight of apples were removed from the trees. One luckless individual, who had lost his entire yield of particularly choice pears, advertised in the Press that they had been sprayed with arsenic. The only consideration which this humane warning obtained for him was that, on the night following the publication of his advertisement, his entire crop of apples disappeared in their turn. But potatoes exercised the chief attraction.

What made potato thieving the more serious and exasperating was the fact that its unchecked continuance rendered the premature lifting of the crop imperative in order that some of it might be saved from the marauders. Unfortunately, their unripe condition was bound to have the serious effect that, stored for winter consumption, the potatoes would not keep, thus still further reducing the amount reckoned upon for the rationed supply of the people.

To make matters worse for the civil population, as military rations were perforce reduced, the troops received increases of pay in order to enable them to purchase supplementary food in the shops, markets and on the farms. At the same time, an Order was published limiting the amount of such purchases to a fair and reasonable quantity, but not the slightest notice was taken of this Order. These men, obviously entrusted by their respective messes with money, would enter business premises and the markets in small squads, violently elbow aside civilian purchasers and buy up whole stocks of the exposed commodities. The salesmen and women, overawed by their loud-mouthed insistence, were too terrified to refuse to sell, as they had a perfect right to do, the result being that, over and over again, civilians, often helpless women, were compelled, not always with success, to seek their requirements elsewhere.

As the end of the year drew nearer, the German Authorities began to view with disapproval the fact that town dwellers still found occasional means of supplementing their meagre rations by such additions as small quantities of unmilled wheat, butter, eggs, milk and other foodstuffs procured from friends in the country districts. They, therefore, on a well remembered Saturday, posted squads of men on the roads leading to St. Helier with instructions to halt all wayfarers carrying bags or packages, and to examine the contents of all vehicles. Even baskets attached to the handle-bars of bicycles were inspected, and all foodstuffs were seized; identity-cards were taken, and their unfortunate owners were warned to appear before the German Authorities to account for the possession of the articles detained.

In some cases, where the explanation was deemed satisfactory, the goods were returned in whole or in part; but in others they were arbitrarily confiscated, and the owners were heavily fined for being in possession of rationed food in excess of the prescribed amount. The seizure of eggs was particularly gratuitous, as these, with leaf tobacco also seized, were not rationed at all.

About this time, the Occupying Authority, having learned that Jersey possessed a surplus of slightly over one thousand head of cattle, lost no time in notifying the competent Department that, for the use of the troops in the Island, a provision of seven and a half tons of meat per week would be required. This, of course, necessitated the slaughter of the beautiful little Jersey cattle, for so long a pure and separate breed. However, as the requisition had the appreciable effect of restoring to the civil population a weekly instead of the long-suffered fortnightly four-ounce meat ration, the matter was received with placid composure.

The fact that the adjacent Normandy coast was by this time in the possession of the Allies stimulated a new and interesting development, namely, a number of attempts, for the most part made by adventurous young men, to escape from Jersey and to reach the French coast, only some fifteen miles distant. At a much earlier period, one or more such ventures had proved successful, even while France remained in German hands, the daring fugitives being picked up at sea by one or other of our patrol vessels. Chances of success, however, were so remote that few cared to take them, while failure resulted in severe prison penalties. But from the date of the presence so close at hand, of units of the Allied Forces, interest in the more promising possibilities of escape revived, and several small craft, borrowed or commandeered for the purpose, managed to negotiate by night the short sea-voyage across to Normandy.

The young men who courageously took their lives in their

hands in these attempts to reach France and England, certainly ran risks grave enough to deter most people. In the first place numerous German sentries on coast patrol duty had to be evaded. Secondly, the treacherous ocean currents, of great swiftness and strength, which sweep past the rock-strewn channels surrounding the Island, rendered a close study of tides imperative. Thirdly, German patrol boats were on the watch. Last but not least, arrangement for departure had to be made after curfew, when interference from land patrols might be looked for everywhere.

One of these bold attempts unhappily failed owing to the development of a leak which, on the speedy filling of the somewhat ancient and decrepit craft, necessitated a lengthy swim back to the point of departure and the capture of all hands on landing. Another attempt was discovered by the coast patrol at the moment of launching the boat. In this case, one of the adventurers, quite a youth, was shot dead, and his companions in misfortune arrested. This melancholy incident naturally discouraged further attempts, and for some time no evasions were planned, an additional difficulty being placed in the way by the publication of a German Order peremptorily warning civilians off all the Island beaches, under penalty, *inter alia*, of being fired upon without challenge.

Disregarding this warning, another attempt was attended by a shocking tragedy. In November 1944, two young men and a married couple only a few months wedded, seeking to escape in boisterous weather, were driven upon the rocks, and all four lost their lives within sight of the Island.

But quite a number succeeded in making good their escape. I think it was calculated that, up to the date last mentioned, between fifty and sixty brave youths between the ages of 18 and 25 had succeeded in eluding the vigilance of the patrols and sentries and escaping to the French coast. But even those who failed to reach England and join the Forces (the goal of nearly all of them), gave proof of great courage and strength of purpose. Those who failed earned and received both sympathy and admiration.

During 1944, on a number of occasions, the bodies of

British bluejackets, from our small ships sunk in the neighbouring seas were washed ashore on the Jersey coasts. They were buried with full naval honours, the German troops in occupation providing bearers and firing parties. The interments took place in a cemetery specially consecrated; well-constructed crosses of seasoned oak recording the names and ratings of the deceased in so far as they were ascertainable. These graves were tended and cared for in turn by the boys and girls of various schools in the Island, who willingly undertook this kindly duty.

About the same time, a number of prisoners of the American Army, who had been captured by the Germans about the date of the fall of St. Malo, were brought to Jersey and confined in the barracks on the summit of Fort Regent. I believe these numbered twenty-one, and included three officers, of whom one was a Colonel. Their capture evoked much sympathy among the Jersey people, and every effort was made, by means of the provision of small comforts and additional food, to render their wearisome confinement more bearable. This, at a time when we were all suffering from the stringency imposed by our small rations, was no easy task; but the response to an appeal privately launched was wonderful. The farmers sent so many eggs and fowls and so much butter, and the ladies of the Island, including many young girls in business employment, provided so many cakes and delicacies, that the imprisoned Americans were almost overwhelmed by the spate of good things that daily rained in on them. For American Thanksgiving Day, a small fund was started and quickly subscribed to give them a turkey and plum-pudding dinner which came to them as a complete and welcome surprise. Everyone to whom application was made did his or her best to improve the lot of the unfortunate men who showed great and touching appreciation for everything that was done for them.

Towards the end of the year, or early in 1945, two of the officers, a Captain and a Subaltern, escaped. What actually happened to them was never known; but it was whispered that they had succeeded in getting clear away from the Island.

After the Allied Invasion of Normandy, for some reason

which was never explained, the public were suddenly and without warning deprived of the use of their telephones. It is difficult to afford any idea of the dislocation and disturbance which this harsh, inconsiderate and unnecessary German Order caused to nearly everybody. It was felt seriously enough by professional, commercial and business men; but equally exasperating was its effect upon private householders. In cases of sudden illness, particularly in the country districts, inability quickly to summon medical aid was attended in numbers of cases by serious results, while inability to call the Police or Fire Fighting Services, caused much anxiety. To seek help of any kind after the hour of curfew, through pitch dark streets or country roads, liable at any moment to be halted by armed enemy patrols incapable of understanding explanations, presented a prospect of delay in which valuable time might be lost and life and property gravely endangered. These, however, were considerations which apparently did not occur to the Teutonic mind.

After a lapse of about two months the use of the telephone was restored; but only from 8 a.m. to 8.30 p.m., a limitation which still left the civil population unprovided with ready means of communication during the hours of darkness when, often, it was most urgently needed.

But, from a very early period of the German Occupation, you were liable at any moment to be deprived of the use of your telephone. It appeared that, to supply all military needs, there was a shortage of instruments. When, therefore, any new German Department was established, or private house requisitioned for the use of some officer or official, the nearest premises were liable to be coolly entered and have the telephone carried off without the smallest apology or explanation. More often than not the instruments were never returned.

To complete each newly established telephone communication, streets, roads and houses were quickly festooned with lines, hastily and primitively suspended. These frequently passed across your front windows, hitched on to the shutters, the lines sagging in an unsightly and slovenly manner. But in no circumstances might they be touched; to do so was to risk a charge of sabotage and liability of death.

About the middle of January 1945, we finally lost all use of our telephones. Thenceforward to the end of the war, telephonic communication in the Island did not exist.

CHAPTER FOUR

THE STATES ASSEMBLY

I THINK that it is desirable at this point, in order that the attitude of the States Assembly of the Island of Jersey towards the Germans may be clearly understood by readers of this book in the United Kingdom and elsewhere, to give some account of that body. For many years past, Island administration has been widely regarded in Jersey as antiquated, although there have been some recent proposed reforms.

The administration of the Island of Jersey is conducted by a kind of insular parliament called The States. This assemblage is composed of no less than 53 persons, namely, 12 Jurats, 12 Rectors, 12 Constables and 17 Deputies. It is an Assembly whose independence has long been recognised, and is presided over by the Bailiff, the chief magistrate and head of the Island Government. However, the Bailiff possesses no administrative powers except by and through the States, which body is further reinforced by an Attorney-General, exercising the functions of Public Prosecutor, a Solicitor-General, a Viscount who acts as Sheriff and Coroner, a Receiver-General, a Greffier or States Registrar, and one or two minor officials.

The curious spectacle thus presents itself of a little island in the English Channel, with an area considerably smaller than the private estates of many English and Scottish landowners and with the population of a fifth-rate English Provincial town, having an Assembly numbering a round dozen more members than that of the State Council of the Island of Ceylon with its area of 25,332 square miles, and its population of five and a half millions.

The Bailiff is not only President of the States; he is, in

addition, as first magistrate of the Island, Chief (and only) Justice of the Royal Court. This appointment carries with it a salary of £2,000 a year, and is made by the Home Office in London. It is one to which the Attorney-General usually but not invariably succeeds.

The offices of Attorney-General and Solicitor-General, formerly designated *Procureur Général* and *Avocat Général*, are of great antiquity. These officials may be called upon, as in other lands, to furnish opinions upon any legal or constitutional point which may arise. In the Royal Court it is the Attorney-General, in his capacity as Public Prosecutor, who proceeds against the delinquent and recommends the penalty. This penalty, recommended by him, is called his Conclusion; it must be received and accepted or modified before the Court can pronounce sentence. The Attorney-General, in addition, is head of the Honorary Police of the Island, over which Force, however, he has little direct control. The salaries of the Attorney-General and Solicitor-General are £1,100 and £700 a year respectively.

The origin of the title of Viscount is traceable back to about the middle of the twelfth century when Jersey was regarded as a portion of the Duchy of Normandy and the Duke's representative was known as the Viscomte. The post has diminished in importance, so that it now ranks after that of Attorney-General. The Viscount's duties have already been stated; he is *ex-officio* a member of the States, although possessing neither vote nor right of speech.

The twelve Jurats are elected for life by the votes of the entire Island. This is a great weakness. Fortunately, at the time of writing, proposals to reform this archaic system have recently been laid before the Home Office. Long-standing discontent should be removed by the proposal to limit tenure of office by these men to six years with eligibility thereafter for re-election. Reform was long overdue; for the Jurats—from the Norman-French *Juré Justicier*, meaning sworn judge or justiciary—who are members of both the States and the Royal Court, whereto all important cases are remitted by the Stipendiary Magistrate's tribunal, have often had no more than a smattering of legal knowledge.

Aspiring Jurats require only two qualifications: that they be Jersey-born, and that they possess property amounting in value to the equivalent of forty quarters of wheat-rent, which I understand to be worth about £30 a year. Jurats receive no salary or emoluments, and are bound to attend meetings of the States, unless sick, under penalty of a fine. Their appointment is looked upon as conferring high honour, and competition, on vacancies arising has at times been keen. That it should be considered an honour is scarcely surprising when we consider the importance attached to them. But experience shows that the best type of man is not always chosen; indeed, many incompetent choices have been made. However worthy as an individual the average Jurat may be, he is, I should imagine, scarcely of the material of which, in other lands, jurists and law-givers are usually composed.

The twelve Rectors are the incumbents of the twelve parishes into which the Island is divided. With their Dean, who is President of the Local Ecclesiastical Court, they also are appointed for life. They too must be of Jersey birth, their livings being under the patronage of the Crown on presentation by the Bishop of Winchester in whose diocese Jersey has for centuries been placed.

Some of these clerics have been very old for administrators. That they should continue to be members of the States at all has for long been a matter of widespread condemnation. The view is held by all classes that Rectors possess little or no qualification for duties of a legislative character for which, it is considered, they are for the most part unfitted. Rectors as statesmen, it is now thought, fulfil little or no useful purpose and, of recent years, whatever may have been the case formerly, have proved something of a drag on the administrative machine.

Another welcome reform, however, will shortly deprive them of their age-old privilege of *ex-officio* right to membership of the States Assembly. Rectors will, I understand, be permitted, however, to offer themselves for election as Deputies.

The acceptance by the States of this and like reforms is the outcome of an agitation which for some time past has convulsed the Island. But the agitation has had good results. If the reforms are accepted, statesmen, many of whom in the past have displayed but limited intelligence and little qualification, may in the course of time give place to those with more vigorous mental processes, with greater knowledge of the world and a wider comprehension of their responsibilities to the public whom they have undertaken to serve.

The twelve Constables or *Connétables* have no English equivalent. These parish officials are selected usually from the ranks of the farmer or tradesman class. They are elected for a limited period and their appointments are entirely honorary. In addition to being a member of the States, a Constable fulfils the duties of chief administrative officer in his parish; he is also head of the local honorary Police. His magisterial powers are confined to summary settlement of petty disputes and the infliction of small fines. He is chairman of the Parish Council or Committee entrusted with the assessment and collection of the rate. A Constable may, in addition, hold preliminary enquiries into infractions of the law and remit delinquents to the Stipendiary Magistrate's Court of St. Helier.

The seventeen Deputies, also elected for limited periods of office, are similarly members of the States. Deputies are a comparatively recent addition to the Chamber, having been first added in 1856. They are understood generally to safeguard the interests of the commercial classes, from which they are chiefly drawn, and to keep a close watch for the purpose of protecting themselves and their constituents against any inroads into their liberties and interests which might result from unconsidered measures introduced into the States by their brethren the Jurats, Rectors and Constables.

Legislation of the States must be submitted to and confirmed by His Majesty's Privy Council before reaching the local Statute Book. Acts of the British Parliament do not become operative in Jersey until extended to the Island by order in Council and registered in the Royal Court at St. Helier.

After the outbreak of war in 1939, the various Committees

of the States, responsible for the life and well-being of the people, were temporarily transformed into Departments. These, eight in number, bore the following names: Transport and Communications, Finance and Economics, Agriculture, Public Health, Essential Services, Essential Commodities, Public Instruction and Labour. Each of these Departments was placed in the charge of a Jurat as President with two consultants. These eight Presidents, with the Bailiff and Crown officials, were formed into a body known as the Superior Council, which discharged useful duties in receiving and discussing proposals which, on acceptance, were embodied in bills for submission to full sittings of the States. It fulfilled other functions of a consultative character as well, and might, in a word, have been described as a kind of Council of Advice.

There was, in my opinion, an attempt by the Departments unduly to centralise everything in their own hands. Many irritating decrees made life more difficult. Life generally was admittedly not easy; but clumsy interferences, such as the attempt to centralise distribution of clothing and other things in the hands of officialdom, however well-intentioned, were often a nuisance.

From time to time small supplies of clothing and material were purchased in France and imported into Jersey by a public Department. But there was never enough to go round. On their release, queues of people waited wearily for the doors to open, often for many hours and not infrequently in the cold and wet, and went away empty-handed.

On one occasion, which will serve as an illustration of the chaotic situation, I spent one hour and three-quarters outside an otherwise completely empty shoemaker's establishment awaiting my turn to acquire, on presentation of the relevant coupons cut from my Textile Ration Book, two pairs of shoe laces of which a much needed supply had been received from France. There was an easier way, however, of obtaining goods —if one had influence!

Exorbitant prices were demanded for goods imported by the States, and often non-essential commodities were brought in while many were suffering from miserably short commons of bread and other food-stuffs. Red wine, even when heavily diluted, sweetened with saccharine, and in none too pure or clean a condition, often resulted in serious gastric disorders—but one could always produce a medical certificate for a bottle of bad brandy at a price which eventually rose to over forty-eight shillings a bottle! But perhaps the wine was introduced to take the minds of the people off their sufferings.

Farmers probably suffered most from the various decrees and regulations. Their lives, already difficult under German rule as previously described, were made even more difficult. There can be no doubt that, during the German occupation, farmers were constantly harassed in the pursuit of their important industry. One would have supposed that, in view of the necessities of the community as a whole every possible facility and encouragement would have been afforded them. Instead, from 1940 onward, the farmer, not in all cases an individual capable of readily comprehending the often complicated demands issued to him, was forced to spend much time which might otherwise have been more profitably employed in filling up lengthy declarations and returns of doubtful value. In conformity with these, as a few examples only, he was compelled to observe all kinds of formalities in relation to the delivery of his milk; to report immediately the acquisition, sale, loss or slaughter of his animals; not to lift, sort or dispose of his potato crop without permission, often withheld or cancelled without rhyme or reason at the moment when his hired helpers had arrived; to sell to the Department concerned all crops of cereals and potatoes at stated prices, which crops he might not thresh except under States supervision; to sell garden produce only on the land producing it; to make periodical returns of all fowls and poultry under two years of age; to slaughter, without adequate compensation, all calves fourteen days after birth; to report all calvings (except in special unspecified circumstances) within 48 hours; to abstain, under penalty, from selling potatoes or cereals to any person whomsoever, and to dispose of his entire crop, as stated at specified prices, to a States Department; to give immediate notice of the births of all pigs and calves and (again) to furnish accurate returns of every description of live-stock (cats and dogs excepted) on his premises; to mark his cattle, and to abstain from moving them from one place to another over imaginary lines drawn across the Island unless furnished with special permits the provision of which, if granted, took up much valuable time and involved unnecessary and unremunerative labour.

The foregoing comprise only a few of the numberless Orders and Regulations issued by the States to farmers in Jersey. As a whole they were curious and annoying examples of tiresome and often useless complexity.

Penalties inflicted upon farmers by the States officials for the slightest derogation or omission to carry out these Orders and Regulations were unduly heavy. Some may have been justified, but farmers were treated more harshly than other sections of the community, as witness the following random examples:

August 30th, 1940. An unfortunate man, who had purchased a cow, was fined £12 and £2 costs for making a little butter without a permit from the Department of Agriculture. He was perfectly unconscious of any necessity to obtain such a permit. He had made the butter for his own use, and like an honest man, had refrained from drawing his butter ration during its consumption.

June 3rd, 1942. A farmer was fined £100 and £10 costs for omitting to send a small quantity of milk to the Department concerned.

January 11th, 1943. A farmer was fined £50 and £10 costs for threshing a small quantity of his own wheat.

August 28th, 1943. For omitting to register pigs in his possession, a farmer was fined £6.

On the same day, for carelessly signing a declaration relating to potatoes in his possession, an offender was fined £100.

September 3rd, 1943. For abstracting a portion of the cream from his milk, a dairyman was fined £100 and £20 costs.

On the 23rd of the same month, for omitting to declare the birth of a litter of pigs within the prescribed period of 48 hours and for having a sow in his possession without a permit, a farmer was fined £70 and £20 costs.

December 5th, 1943. For neglecting to register three calves, a farmer was fined £75 and £10 costs.

January 8th, 1944. For having in his possession five undeclared pigs, a farmer was fined £200 and £10 costs, a purely technical offence for which, on the same day, two other persons were each fined £60.

In the month of March 1944, for killing a horse and selling its perfectly wholesome meat, apparently without specifying the nature of such meat, a seller was fined £500.

CHAPTER FIVE

RATIONING

EARLY in the month of July 1940, and soon after the arrival in the Island of the German Forces, general rationing was introduced. The first weekly adult scale was announced as follows: Meat 12 oz. (including a proportion of fat and bone), Butter 4 oz., sugar 4 oz. Bread, milk and potatoes were not yet rationed.

When one looked back, a couple of years later, at the exuberant liberality of these quantities, one wondered what on earth we did with all that food, for, as will soon be seen, such astonishing liberality was short lived. Ten days after the introduction of the system, the States published an Order that, for the purpose of checking *hoarding,* the public were forbidden to purchase more supplies of food than were necessary for seven days' consumption.

A week later, the allowance per week of cooking fat, which had been tentatively fixed at 4 oz., was hastily halved, while, a few days later, tea was issued on the scale of 4 oz. per person, an issue destined to be of short duration. On August 3rd, two meatless days, Thursday and Friday in one week, were ordered. On those days the cooking or consumption of meat became a penal offence. Exception was made in the case of horse-flesh, birds and rabbits, but the luxury of horseflesh had not yet been made available, fowls were rarities, whilst rabbits, already changing hands as from 25s. to 35s. each, were not likely to be of more than strictly limited use.

So, on a *régime* of two and two-fifths ounces of meat (with bone) per day for five days out of seven, the general public of Jersey were bidden cheerfully and hopefully to look to the future strong in' the comforting reflection that bread, vegetables and potatoes at any rate remained plentiful, and that there was still a satisfactory supply of milk.

But these luxurious conditions prevailed in the far off days of 1940. Later, the daily ration of meat, if available, was nine drachms, or just over half an ounce, including bone.

On February 1st, 1941, bread having been added to the list of rationed foods, adults receiving 4 lb. 10 oz. per week, except heavy industrial workers who were granted slightly more, a new scale was issued as follows:

	British		Germans	
Bread	4 lb. 10	oz.	5 lb. 2½	oz.
Meat	12	"	16	"
Butter	2	"	5	"
Cooking fat	2	"	2	"
Sugar	4	"	6	"
Tea	2	"	2	"
Flour	4	"	6	"
Salt	2	"	2	"

On March 2nd, the issue of cooking fat to British consumers was stopped; the only method of preparing the daily meat course was, therefore, by some form of boiling. The week's meat ration-card was divided into eight spaces providing for one and a half ounces each, this, as the official notice stated, being 'considered as the quantity of meat required for eight meat meals.'

In an effort to enable the working classes to make the most of this nourishment an establishment called the Sun Works was commissioned, to supply a meat and vegetable stew in glass containers at a cost of threepence per half pint. The public, however, did not find this preparation to their taste; so the experiment did not last long. Soon afterwards, a communal kitchen was opened which supplied simple meals at a reasonable charge. It was well supported and greatly appreciated.

About this time, enquiries of a somewhat pointed character, were printed in letters to the Press. These sought information as to the mysterious disappearance from the *abattoir* of steaks, sirloins, and the choicer cuts of the slaughtered beasts, as these, it was pointed out, were never to be seen either in the market or in the shops of retailers. That there were adequate reasons for these letters, the following anecdotes, which have been vouched for, will clearly show.

In a wellknown and popular hairdressing establishment in St. Helier, two young men of respectable appearance, seated side by side as they awaited vacant chairs, exchanged somewhat outspoken views on prevailing conditions. Meanwhile, his back view alone visible to them, head bowed upon his chest and swathed in white coverings, a prominent personage submitted to the ministrations of the operating artist.

'Do themselves well?' said one of the waiting men blissfully unaware of the ownership of the opulent back upon which his eyes were fixed. 'You're telling me. Them States people live on the fat of the land. They get their joints of meat for Sunday's dinner all right.' Here the owner of the opulent back might have been observed to stiffen. 'I could tell you a thing or two. Yes, and you and me on our twelve ounces of meat a week. Pretty thick, I call it.'

A few moments later, the overweight listener rose rather ponderously to his feet, and glared down at the unconcerned speaker, who coolly returned his angry gaze.

'You know perfectly well,' he thundered, 'that what you have just been saying is absolutely false.'

'Oh, no, it's not,' coolly replied the other. 'What I've told my friend is perfectly true, and wot's more I can prove it. Look 'ere. You are ——, aren't you? You get your meat from ——, don't you? Well, I'm the assistant wot cuts your joints for you every week. I know wot you get. Last week you 'ad four pounds of ribs of beef and two pounds of steak, now, 'adn't you? You needn't try that game on with me, for I know. See?'

From a dusky red, the discomfited personage's face quickly assumed the hue of a ripe tomato as, muttering unintelligibly, he snatched up his hat and stick and made for the street, followed by the unchecked merriment of the delighted assistants.

'You didn't ought to have said that, George,' feebly remonstrated the speaker's companion, as the former moved towards the vacated chair.

'W'y not?' asked the other with a grin. ' 'E knows it's true enough. . . . Gone to get me the sack, 'as 'e? Oh well, that don't matter much to me. I sacked myself this mornin' and go to a better job on Monday, so 'e'll find 'isself pushed when he gets there. 'Air-cut and shampoo, please.'

The foregoing side-light on the private life of a well-known Jerseyman was gleefully retailed to me by a perfectly reliable witness of the scene as it actually took place.

The feast of Nöel in each year of the German Occupation, although it lacked its customary good cheer in the homes of the rationed public, fell short of little of its traditional plenty in the dwellings of those who took advantage of their position. On Christmas Day, 1942, rationing being then much more stringent than at the outset of its introduction, a friend of the writer was bidden to a high tea party at the house of a certain well-known islander. The table, with its festive, holly-decked plates of sandwiches, hot scones swimming in butter, mince-pies and iced cakes, certainly conveyed no hint of either rationing or other form of comestible stringency. The host and hostess were well-to-do, homely people, ceremony was banished, and when, at a given moment, the substantial beef sandwiches, greatly favoured, showed signs of running low, the jovial, well-fed master of the house loudly called to a waiting maid to BRING IN THE JOINT AND CUT SOME MORE. This was done, to the round-eyed amazement of the guests who, painfully subsisting on their four ounces of meat a week, gazed wonderingly and enviously upon the noble sirloin which speedily made its appearance upon the polished sideboard.

On another occasion a little later, a very prominent member of Jersey society was surprised, seated at the mid-day dinner table, operating enthusiastically upon a nicely roasted leg of pork.

At the end of April 1941, the weekly meat ration for adults was reduced from 12 oz. to 8 oz., for children to 4 oz., and for Germans to 10 oz., while, in the following month, a further reduction was ordered to 4 oz., 2 oz. and 5 oz. respectively.

The ration of meat remained at that scale for several years, except on those not infrequent occasions when there was no issue of meat at all. From mid-Summer of the same year, issues of meat took place on alternate weeks only, there being a slight increase in the butter ration in the weeks when the meat failed.

Bread was first rationed in February 1941. In the previous August, white flour being still available, bread was ordered to contain not more than 21 nor less than 19 parts of mashed potatoes. Loaves now became so heavy as to be positively inedible. Small 1 lb. loaves could not be successfully utilised for the morning exercises by persons unprovided with dumb-bells, and several bakers' delivery vans were said to have been sent to the garage suffering from strained chassis and broken spring-leaves.

About the same time, the baking of rolls, buns, cakes and fancy pastry was sternly forbidden. Later, in 1941, white flour being no longer obtainable by the masses, wholemeal was employed for bread making. Against this, of course, nobody could legitimately complain; but unhappily for the consumers of the resulting bread, this flour was allowed to pass to the bakers in a lamentably impure condition. It contained husks, pieces of straw and string, fragments of gunnybag, even match-stems, as well as other objects not usually encountered in the daily loaf.

The immediate and widespread result took the form of an epidemic of what came to be called Jerseyitis, a new and severe form of stomach disorder, long a source of serious tribulation.

In July 1941, the weekly bread ration was reduced to 4 lb. 8 oz. for adults, or a shade more than 10 oz. per day. Men in the heavy industries were granted 6 lb. per week, women receiving 5 lb. 12 oz. When it is borne in mind that men in H.M. Forces receive 1 lb. of bread per day, and vagrants in English Poor Law Institutions still more, the insufficiency of the allowance will be readily appreciated. With 4 oz. of meat per week, in spite of a sufficiency of potatoes, such a *régime* was clearly too low to enable normal health to be maintained, and slowly but surely as time went on, vitality waned and the effect of the general food insufficiency became more and more apparent in the faces and figures of the people.

Two or three times, during the years of the German Occupation, to supplement the ration of bread, an issue of hard ship's biscuits was made. Eight ozs. per adult was the allowance; but this exercised little effect in alleviating the pangs of hunger from which the great majority of Jersey people already continuously suffered.

On January 11th, 1941, in order to enable the States to lower the small subsidy which they paid to keep down the price of the loaf, an official notice appeared begging the people to eat potatoes as far as possible, in place of bread. It is not known to what extent this request was complied with.

The above bread ration continued until, in May 1943, the issue was reduced from 4 lb. 8 oz. to 3 lb. 12 oz. per week, or a shade over 8 oz. per day. By that time, as will be described later, potatoes were also rationed, only 5 lb. per week being allowed to each adult person. It will thus be observed that the health of the public was to be maintained on a daily food allowance of 9 drachms of meat, 8 oz. of bread and about 11 oz. of potatoes. These three items formed, as it were, the daily alimentary sheet anchor for, truth to tell, there was very little else. Vegetables were often hard to come by, and at best contained nothing in the way of sustaining nutrition. Eggs had disappeared; the Germans saw to that. Rabbits and fowls, of which there were very few and when available worth almost their weight in gold, were far beyond the means of any but the wealthy. Small wonder then that these rations, to which were added 2 oz. of butter and 3 oz. of sugar weekly caused the Black Market to flourish. One either paid extra or starved with the unfortunate poor.

The public, as a whole, could only tighten their belts and suffer in silence; but some there were who, during the long and cheerless period through which we passed, lacked hardly anything. Without question, these men and women possessed private sources of supply of all kinds of provisions and liquor. The healthy vigour of their well-nourished bodies provided a striking contrast to the hunger-produced emaciation now only too apparent in the faces and figures of the general public. Many of the latter, pinched by privation and sheer want, daily roamed the streets and markets, their once well-fitting clothing hanging upon them, searching wistfully but vainly for food.

For many years the Island of Jersey had been deservedly famous for the excellence of its potatoes; farmers raised a surprising quantity when regard is had to the limited acreage available for their cultivation. A year or two before the outbreak of war, the value of Jersey potatoes exported to English markets, after providing for the needs of an insular population of about 45,000, exceeded a million pounds sterling. Although, soon after the German Occupation, a certain proportion of arable land was devoted to the raising of cereal crops, there still remained, for local needs, more than enough for the cultivation of the invaluable tuber. Nevertheless in the month of December 1941, we find the States, to the amazement of the public, issuing a warning foreshadowing an unanticipated need for the introduction of potato rationing.

For this, there were two reasons: the considerable quantity consumed by the German troops, and the appalling waste arising from the unchecked local manufacture of a substance called potato-flour.

When, soon after the disappearance of white wheat-flour, some person discovered and announced in the Press that it was possible, though at the expense of much labour and many potatoes, to fabricate a substitute from the Island's staple crop, the method described was everywhere enthusiastically adopted. Members of those departments of the States, who should at once have taken steps to check the deplorable wastage, did nothing, although warnings of a resultant shortage were published in the local newspaper. I believe that I am right in saying that from twelve to fourteen pounds of potatoes are required to produce one pound of this flour. One needs, therefore, but little imagination to estimate the effect of this scandalous abuse when it is realised that almost every family in the Island immediately set to work to supply itself with such an inexpensive and appreciable luxury.

Potato-flour was once utilised in all sorts of ways from the making, in combination with other substances, of puddings, biscuits and cakes, to the thickening of vegetable soups and the composition of milk puddings. It soon became a remunerative industry and, costing about eighteen pence, was speedily on sale at from four to six shillings a pound. Soon mechanical and electrical energy were used to speed up production and increase output, with a result which any person of ordinary intelligence could easily have foreseen.

In December 1941, the States awoke from their potato-flour-produced lethargy, and, realising dimly at length the straits to which, through their own heedless inaction, the Island was now reduced, and with a view to the introduction of some scheme of rationing, appealed to growers of potatoes to sell to the Department of Agriculture all stocks in their possession. They likewise ordered the public to send to that Department returns of all potatoes held by them. In addition, inspectors were appointed to visit private premises and report the results of their inspections. But neither then nor thereafter did the States seriously attempt to check the manufacture of potato-flour. It is, perhaps, only fair to recall that, already in the month of November 1941, in a feeble effort to check potato wastage the public were implored, in a published notice, to refrain from peeling their potatoes, and to consume them complete with skins intact.

Finally potatoes were rationed on a basis of 10 lb. per adult per week, and this, all things considered, was a fair and reasonable allowance. How, in those conditions, it was found possible to continue the fabrication of potato-flour cannot be explained; but continue it most assuredly did. In August 1942, the potato ration was reduced from 10 lb. to 5 lb. and on February 27th following, the Department of Agriculture having apparently neglected full precautions in carrying out its storage arrangements, the Superior Council appealed to the 'generosity' of an already half-starved populace to return to the Department of Agriculture 'surpluses of potatoes' held. At the same time, the Council intimated, if this were not done, that it would still further reduce the 5 lb. weekly ration, or, pending the lifting of the 1943 crop some months later, leave the people without any potatoes at all. This, of course, would have meant widespread and utter starvation for many.

And now the public of Jersey began to realise what hunger and privation really meant. Storage had been so faulty that a great portion of the residue of the 1942 crop had rotted, with the result that, when issued, nearly fifty per cent. of one of the people's principal articles of daily food was found to be unfit for consumption.

But still the public struggled on, cheered by the hope that the 1943 crop would perhaps suffice to enable rationing of potatoes to be discontinued. That comforting anticipation might in all probability have been realised had not the Germans stepped in. No sooner was the 1943 crop lifted than the Civil Commandant proceeded to requisition great quatities for export to the Continent, and day by day and week by week the spectacle of the shipment of hundreds, indeed thousands of tons of the people's food was bitterly witnessed. The daily ration of eleven ounces (5 lb. per week) had, therefore, perforce to be continued, and this was with a first rate crop. So hunger, privation and want continued to be bitterly felt, the greatest bitterness residing in the unshakable popular belief that, once again, not the smallest effort had been made to abate or modify a demand whose rapacity was a direct menace to the welfare of many thousands of Jersey people.

Owing to military requirements and other causes, vegetables of all kinds were frequently difficult if not impossible to obtain. As a result of these oft-repeated shortages, we find in the local Press of April 19th, 1941, a strong recommendation to utilise stinging nettles, sorrel, dandelions and bracken. The nettles, it was stated, might be prepared as a spinach, the sorrel stewed to serve as a substitute for cabbage and the bracken boiled and consumed as a kind of imitation asparagus. About this time, probably as the outcome of these experiments, a severe epidemic of colic laid many persons low.

Later in the year, for no intelligible reason, growers of vegetables were ordered to sell their garden produce on their gardens or land only, and were forbidden to open places of business for that purpose without a special licence from the

Food Control.

In Jersey we had always possessed plenty of milk. The Island milk is probably as rich in cream as any in the world, and, for that reason alone, Jersey cattle have at all times been highly esteemed. The supply of milk, therefore, from the outbreak of war to the German Occupation, never ran short. Some time after that event, however, owing no doubt to extensive German consumption, deliveries to the public were limited to one pint per head each day, and, on the whole, that quantity was found to be sufficient. On August 29th, 1941, however, the milk ration was suddenly reduced to half a pint for adults and one pint for growing children. This step was taken by the Department concerned for reasons which were never made clear. It was supposed that the reduction related to the necessity for making more butter; but as the weekly ration of two ounces was not increased, there must have been some other reason behind the Order which it was not considered convenient to publish. Milk, moreover, had to be delivered by farmers to certain designated centres of distribution, under pain of heavy penalties. This Order gave rise to much unnecessary inconvenience. In addition, the public were advised that skim milk would be on sale at various named dairies.

The outcome of this intimation was that, long before the dairies opened their doors, long queues of patient women, milk-jug in hand, waited in all weathers to purchase the greatly desired milk. Again and again, owing entirely to lack of organisation, the quantity available was nothing like sufficient for the needs of the hopeful applicants with the result that scores of disappointed people, after waiting for hours, often had perforce to return empty-handed to their homes. This was just one more instance of official heedlessness and want of regard for the convenience of the lower classes, who were not permitted to leave their receptables to be filled before the dairy opened and to send for them later.

It will have been observed that no mention has hitherto been made of eggs. From very early in the occupation of Jersey, eggs completely disappeared from the trade of St. Helier. Germans in motor-cars commandeered them from the farms so systematically that few, if any, ever reached the town. It was thus with the utmost difficulty that small supplies could be reserved for hospitals and nursing homes. Finally, at prices of anything from three to four shillings *each*, eggs were very occasionally offered for sale in the Black Market. A few farmers there were, however, who reserved eggs for their friends and for invalids at a reasonable price, and, by so doing, earned the deep gratitude of those who benefited by their benevolence.

In June 1942, fish was rationed for the first time, the public being instructed to register with fishmongers for that purpose. From July 16th, 1940, control of all ports and harbours was vested in the Occupying Authority, and, thenceforward, and following each other at frequent intervals, Orders, relating particularly to fishing-boats, rendered fishing both difficult and complicated. The result of these Orders was that, after the satisfaction of German demands, little or no fish remained for the Jersey people. Even at those seasons of the year when the surrounding waters were alive with mackerel, mullet, white-bait and other fish, the man in the street would repair in vain to the retailer with whom he was registered.

At times, during the summer months, a curious crustacean called the spider-crab was on sale at the fishmongers. This remarkable and very aptly-named creature, quite unlike any crab which I had seen elsewhere, a meagre, loose-limbed caricature rather resembling one of those shuddery monsters seen for one horror-stricken moment stealthily approaching you in the helplessness of a disordered dream, held the market for a few short weeks and then disappeared. All that remained thereafter, for most people, were such miserable apologies as limpets and periwinkles, torn maybe from impure rocks; or, for those hardy enough to penetrate the beach land-mines in pursuit of them, sand-eels, razor-fish and ormers, a curious form of oyster. I have been told by people who evidently believed what they were saying that there are methods of preparing ormers for table which transform them into a feast for the gods; but, if that be true, this delicacy is something which I have missed, for the only ormers offered to me were of bouncing resiliency.

If I have perhaps dealt at some length with the food problem, it should be remembered that food occupies a particularly important place in life, especially when it runs short. Let us now examine the plight under German rule of the male and female smoker. The latter, poor soul, we may eliminate from consideration for, from the outset, she was sternly debarred from any participation in daily enjoyment of the cigarette.

On October 28th, 1940, the requirements of male smokers of adult age were provided for as follows: For Jersey and British-born subjects, 20 cigarettes or 5 cigars, or 10 cigarillos (whatever they may have been) or 1 oz. of tobacco *per week*. For Germans, 20 cigarettes or 5 cigars, or 10 cigarillos or 1 oz. of tobacco *per day*. The civilian ration, however, later sank to 20 cigarettes one week and 10 cigarettes together with 1 oz. of tobacco the next.

On November 4th, hundreds of men in lengthy queues haunted all day long the advertised centre of issue for the purpose of obtaining their tobacco ration-cards. They then proceeded to register as customers with selected tobacconists. To the chagrin of the officials of the controlling Department, it was afterwards discovered that, owing to a childishly simple method of verification, many of the applicants, ration-card obtained, walked round the building, re-entered it, approached a different clerk and, without difficulty, secured a second ration-card. Some, indeed, in this way secured several. It was some time before the imposture was brought to light, the discovery providing occasion for much amusement. Only, I think, in one case, was an unlucky delinquent run to earth.

Early in 1941, substitutes for tobacco were timidly and not very enthusiastically experimented with. In the local Press of January 13th we find water-crèss leaves, coltsfoot, the foliage of the blackberry and dried rose petals strongly recommended. With one or other of these, some, bolder than the rest and groping in the dark after new and untried sensations, mingled snuff. This unholy mixture never attained to more than an extremely limited vogue; its sole recommendation being that snuff was at no time rationed.

The tobacco and cigarettes, supplied to the trade from France through a States Department, rapidly deteriorated in quality. As they did so, in equal if not greater measure, they rose in price. As time went on, the appalling rubbish provided was sold when obtainable (and that was not always) at one shilling and ninepence per ounce for the tobacco and one penny each for the cigarettes. I was informed that the prices were fixed by the Department of Essential Commodities, whose buyer purchased the goods in France.

Later, local cultivation of the tobacco plant was successfully undertaken and encouraging results were reported. Apprehension, for some reason, at the widespread adoption by private individuals of this simple solution of their difficulty, a States Department promptly published an order prohibiting the cultivation of tobacco by members of the Jersey public for private consumption except under licence from that Department. But the public were not to be dissuaded. Tobacco planting spread rapidly all over the island. Raised from its own almost microscopical seed and planted out in the Spring, it grew like an enormous weed and without the smallest attention, poor ground being found perfectly suitable for its luxuriant growth and development.

Simple methods of drying and curing the leaf were published in the Press, cutting establishments sprang up, and finally, by the end of 1942, not only was a tobacco, in all respects superior to that supplied at inflated prices by the States, growing freely in almost every garden and in many fields, but large sums were being realised in the Black Market by the sale of the fully prepared tobacco, the disconcerted State officials looking helplessly on.

The Summer months of 1943 saw a still further extension of tobacco cultivation, and now the States took a belated and somewhat speculative hand. They issued an Order laying down that no person, on pain of confiscation, might grow more than one hundred tobacco plants, and, later, that a return showing the exact number grown should be rendered to one of their Departments. I heard that great ingenuity, to bring the vast numbers of plants produced by many growers within the prescribed limit, was displayed in the returns submitted—indeed, immense adroitness must have been displayed, for I heard of no case of confiscation, although, to my own knowledge, some planted fields produced literally thousands of tobacco plants.

In one case, a certain individual planted no less than seventeen thousand plants. An inspector called upon him and demanded to be shown them; his demand was curtly refused. On the official's angry threat to bring the planter before the Court on a charge of obstruction, the latter challenged his visitor to do so, adding that, were the official to carry out his threat, he would make public the names of three Jurats of the Royal Court and two Constables of Parishes who had planted even more than he. Nothing more was heard of the matter.

And now, certain activities of the States in relation to tobacco aroused widespread amusement. It appears that, as the 1943 planting season approached, a local resident, stated to be an expert in tobacco growing and preparation, approached the Superior Council and, with an undertaking to produce a very large quantity of tobacco indeed, applied for the concession of an extensive area of otherwise useless land for the purpose. I assume, although I have no evidence, that some payment was offered. In due course, the application came before the Council. It was gravely considered and unanimously rejected.

But the resourceful applicant was in nowise discouraged. He refused to take no for an answer. Without loss of time he proceeded to lay his plans before the German Authorities. The latter, perceiving at once the advantage to the troops to be derived from a successful realisation of the scheme, immediately granted the application and gave it their whole-hearted support.

When the news reached the Superior Council, the outgeneralled officials realised their mistake. They perceived, all too late, that they should have welcomed the scheme and themselves secured the crop. But was it too late? Hastily, two perturbed and anxious officials waited, hat in hand and perhaps not unmindful of the somewhat humiliating nature of their mission, upon the jubilant planter whose overtures they

93

nad already had a share in declining. In the end, a formal contract was drawn up and signed, the States agreeing to accept the crop of tobacco, no doubt at the grower's price, and to make monetary advances as required to assist him in producing, harvesting and delivering it. It was a complete *volte face*.

This agreement was duly carried into effect and, I understand, advances made totalled the respectable sum of £600. When, however, the leaf was delivered, the departmental officials found to their chagrin that, for one reason or another, it was largely unsuitable for manufacture as a merchantable article. The Department concerned received little sympathy when the facts became known, for recollections of the foul weed of which their costly cigarettes and tobacco had for so long consisted still rankled in the public minds.

But the States were firmly resolved, by some means or other, to get windward of tobacco planters. On December 18th, 1943, a bill was introduced into the Chamber designed heavily to tax tobacco grown for private consumption. By the provisions of this measure, none could be planted without a licence, and each plant grown would be taxed up to a maximum of one shilling. It was estimated that, in that year, owing to the absence of such a tax, at least £10,000 had been lost to revenue. The bill was passed by a large majority.

In the Spring of 1944, the Department of Essential Commodities issued an Order reducing the number of tobacco plants permitted by licence to be grown from one hundred to fifty per person. At the same time, the Department took power to purchase raw leaf at the price of ten shillings a pound, or less if it should so determine. The object of such purchase was, of course, to ration out the product at the controlled price of one Reichsmark (2s. 1½d.) per ounce, thus realising a highly satisfactory profit. Enquiries made the following October, by which time the greater part of the crops of private growers had already been cured and prepared for use, elicited the reluctant information that purchases by the Department had, up to that time, yielded less leaf tobacco than one quarter of the amount required for the issue of a single ration.

At the end of 1944, therefore, the following astonishing situation had arisen. Island grown tobacco, the retail price of which, as we have seen, had been fixed, limited and controlled by the Department of Essential Commodities at one Reichsmark per ounce, had become, for the man in the street, completely unobtainable. The retailing tobacconists had none to sell, for they were unable to procure any stocks from the Department. The reason for this was that, on the one hand, the Department of Essential Commodities, being unable at the price of 10s. per pound to attract sellers, could not supply the trade, while, on the other, growers, each limited by Order to fifty plants, had little or none to spare to the Department. The result was complete deadlock. Tobacconists' shops were empty, while non-tobacco-growing consumers were clamouring for supplies.

By that time, the Department of Essential Commodities must have realised painfully enough that, by fixing an unacceptable purchasing price and, at the same time, limiting production to an absurdly low level, it had not only failed to attract sellers to the Department, but, most unadvisedly, had thrown the limited amount of leaf which should have been available to the trade straight into the hands of the Black Market. Once at the disposal of that enterprising institution, no time was lost in demanding from the public, and especially from the Germans, astronomical prices far in excess of the departmentally controlled limit; the Department, partially responsible for this state of affairs, being completely powerless to check the ramp.

In this way, by a regrettable disregard or ignorance of the immutable laws of cause and effect, of supply and demand, the Department of Essential Commodities not only effectually cut its own throat but ruined the Island trade in tobacco at one and the same time.

I have been informed that, about the end of 1944 and thereafter, tobacco in the Black Market was being sold at prices up to and often exceeding 160 Reichsmarks (£17 per pound) or £1 1s. 3d. per ounce. The yield to States revenue from this commodity in the year we are considering was, of course, hidden from us; but that it reached a total amounting to anything like the £10,000 anticipated is, I should image, exceedingly doubtful.

Early in November, and at lengthy intervals thereafter, the States Department of Essential Commodities did actually issue one or two very small tobacco rations; but this, I learned, was chiefly derived from leaf confiscated from unlicensed growers. The great majority of the civil population was smokeless until the welcome arrival, in January 1945, of a small quantity of cigarettes and tobacco presented by the New Zealand Red Cross.

At an early period of the German Occupation of Jersey, fuel for household purposes became an acute problem. On December 20th, 1940, an Order of the Department of Essential Commodities placed all coal merchants under the necessity of obtaining a departmental licence for the sale for coal and coke. About the same time, deliveries, save in exceptional cases, were limited to prescribed quantities in such a way that not more than one ton could be ordered at a time, that quantity having to serve for a lengthy period. This allowance was not illiberal, but it was soon drastically curtailed. By the early Spring of 1941, the heating of rooms and buildings by means of coal and gas was prohibited; while the use of electricity for fires, radiators, cookers, vacuum cleaners, hairdressers, dentists, or for purposes other than lighting was also sternly forbidden. At mid-Summer, the gas ration, already restricted to certain hours of the day, was again cut by one-third, and water was no longer allowed to be heated by gas.

On December 2nd, 1941, the fuel ration for coal, coke and wood was announced. Householders, irrespective of the size of their house or the number of occupants, received a monthly allocation of half a hundredweight of either coal or coke, and one hundredweight of wood blocks for all purposes. A few weeks later, it was intimated that no future allowance of coal or coke for the heating of rooms or buildings would in any circumstances be made. This was a particularly bitter blow, the more so because the restrictions were not obeyed in the government offices, where enormous fires were often blazing.

Half a hundredweight of coal per month represents approximately one pound and fourteen ounces per day, while one hundredweight of wood blocks consists of about forty-eight of such blocks weighing, on the average, two and one third pounds each. So, if an ordinary householder had, in the coldest winter weather, under two pounds of coal each day, together with about a block and a half of wood, these quantities, with great care and economy, might possibly be made to suffice for about three hours for cooking, heating and everything else.

Consequent upon these rations, the misery and suffering undergone by the citizens of Jersey in the winter months was aggravated. Daily, men and women of all ages and walks of life were to be seen returning to St. Helier laden with branches of trees, or dragging after them perambulators or primitively contrived hand-carts laden with such fuel as they had been able to gather in the surrounding lanes and byways. The wood supplied by the States Distributing Centres at a not inconsiderable cost was both green and wet: possibly the blocks had been soaked to increase their weight; in any event, they were useless as fuel until means could be found to dry them.

Even those who possessed plantations of trees growing in their grounds were not permitted to utilise them for firewood. On July 3rd, 1941, an Order from a States Department prohibited the felling or lopping of trees throughout the island without a formal permit, the Authority reserving to itself the right to requisition, fell and cut up all such trees, both standing and fallen, and to deal with them as it should think fit. The price paid to owners for such timber was, I believe, ten shillings per ton; that charged to consumers of the resulting wood blocks worked out at four pounds fifteen shillings for that quantity.

The general idea behind these measures was apparently to equalise wood distribution for fuel, and I suppose that it was to some extent equalised; but the winter months brought with them a long period of domestic misery, owing to hunger and cold. Neither was easy to bear.

In the last weeks of 1941 a proposal was made to the Bailiff to arrange with the German Authorities for supplies to be imported from Portugal; this was a practical proposal, ensuring a sufficiency of almost every conceivable need in great variety. The Superior Council under the chairmanship of the Bailiff rejected the suggestion. A copy of the proposal will be found in the Appendix at the end of this book.

The scheme, proposed by a person intimately acquainted with Portugal and the country's resources, followed precisely the method pursued by the United States of America when that country, still a neutral, went to the assistance of Belgium in the days of the local food shortage early in the Four Years War, the German Commander-in-Chief in Brussels eagerly agreeing to all the conditions imposed. Had a similar arrangement between Jersey and Portugal been proposed to the German Authorities in the Island, there is no obvious reason why the scheme should not have been gladly authorised and Jersey spared much if not all the want and misery which the people afterwards suffered. Had the results of the disregard with which the proposed Portuguese solution of our difficulties was received by the Superior Council been less tragic, it would have been amusing that the first assistance received by Jersey four years later came precisely from Portugal.

In the preceding pages, readers will have gleaned some idea of what may perhaps be described as the major deprivations to which we were exposed; it may not be without interest if we now consider briefly some of what may be looked upon as our minor unsatisfied wants.

The consumption of tea, if not an absolute necessity, is still dear to the hearts of nearly every Briton, and tea very quickly disappeared, as also did coffee. In the Summer of 1940, soon after the appearance of the Germans in our midst, a weekly ration of 4 oz. of tea was granted by the Food Control. This was reduced in the following October to 2 oz., to 1 oz. in April 1941, while in the following month of July or thereabouts, the leaves of the lime tree, the blackberry and of garden mint were being recommended as palatable substitutes. In October tea was stated to be completely exhausted, and thenceforward, with the substitutes referred to, sugar-beet became the favourite basis for the popular afternoon beverage. But still there seems to have been a fair amount of tea in the Island, for it was even yet, and long thereafter, obtainable—at a price. This price rose steadily until it reached the astronomical figure of twenty pounds sterling per pound in 1943; this figure later reached twenty-five pounds. For coffee, a quite excellent substitute was made by roasting barley.

Sugar, obtainable from France, was, of course, rationed. Unhappily there was no sugar for jam-making; soft fruits, each summer, were, therefore, very largely wasted. But, in spite of the official shortage, sugar, like tea, was still obtainable—at from 15s. to 25s. per pound. Jam, at that figure was therefore, a somewhat expensive luxury. Still, at times, by successfully defying regulations, one might obtain a few pounds of sugar in exchange for a small packet of tea. But most people sweetened their real or imitation coffee with saccharine which arrived occasionally from France. Saccharine tided matters over, more or less, but jam was badly missed. Early in 1942, water, slightly sweetened, was purveyed as 'liquid saccharine.' This was offered to a confiding public at a cost of ninepence per half-pint, and a highly profitable trade would have probably sprung up if the people had been simple-minded enough not to see through the imposture. As it was, the experiment died a speedy death.

Early in April 1941, carrot jam made its appearance. At that time many people still had a certain amount of sugar stowed away and held in reserve. Something was thus produced which at all events facilitated the consumption of the wholemeal bread—and all that it contained.

In July 1941 it was announced that jam would be made in a States-controlled factory and issued to the public as a ration. In this way, about once in five or six weeks, you received a 1 lb. jar of a compound which at any rate tasted sweet. The issues of this somewhat doubtful delicacy, the ingredients and composition of which were not always above suspicion, went on for a long time.

All stocks of wines and spirits held by retailers rapidly passed into German hands, leaving the Island, except for small quantities in private possession, about as dry as the United States in the days of prohibition without the advantage of bootleggers. Wines of all kinds, with the exception of the miserable travesty to which reference has already been made, were no longer obtainable; whisky and gin were mere memories; one probably understands all there is to understand about the brandy except the taste, and that one is mercifully spared; the local breweries were speedily taken over by the German Authorities, and, with material imported by them, brewing of beer went on continuously, but entirely for German benefit. So Jersey went practically dry.

As a whole, we are a cleanly race. We look upon soap, whether for bathroom, wash-hand basin, clothes-washing or floor-scrubbing as a necessity so customary that we cease to consider it any more than the water in which it is used. When, therefore, in February 1941, soap of any kind was no longer obtainable, men and women looked at the shopkeepers and at each other with dismay. But imagination and ingenuity were to come to their aid.

In the local Press of June 20th, selected mud, wood ashes and fine sand were recommended as inexpensive and satisfactory substitutes. Somebody else suggested that, like the Indian Police Officer and his soiled shirt, the human body might be efficiently cleansed by the smart application of a stiff dandy-brush. Some time afterwards, a so-called toilet soap of French manufacture was imported and issued as a ration. This appeared to be made of the selected mud locally recommended. It obstinately refused to lather, and covered your hands with a dusky, malodorous slime. Still, it was theoretically soap; and, as such, entered, under protest as it were, into the daily life of the Island. A ration of a curious cleansing agent of doubtful composition, likewise imported, was utilised for scrubbing purposes, but as all but one of the laundries had been commandeered for the occupying troops and were no longer available for the general public, I am unable to say what was used, apart from chloride of lime, for the usual Monday washing of clothes in those establishments. Later in the Summer of 1944, soap in the Island came completely to an end with serious results; for uncleanliness among workers and their families gave rise to a rapid increase in skin diseases, also to body lice, the well-known carriers of typhus fever.

Of condiments, it was not very long before only salt remained. This took a variety of forms. For a long time only a coarse, crystalline rock-salt was rationed, each person receiving 2 oz. per week. The crystals were of surprising hardness, all attempts to crush them to powder by means of a rolling-pin merely resulting in the utter destruction of the surface of that indispensable implement. The only means of achieving the desired powder, therefore was to borrow an iron mortar and pestle from an obliging chemist.

In August 1942, the only salt obtainable took the disagreeable form of a dreary mixture of salt and earth of indeterminate hue. This had to be immersed in hot water and, on the settlement of the dirt at the bottom of the receptable used, the salt-impregnated liquid was evaporated on the kitchen range. The salt then crystallised on the sides of the vessel, whence it was scraped and came to table.

At the end of 1943, the public were calmly informed that no salt remained in the island, and for some time a States Department arranged for the sale of sea-water from the beaches. This water, costing a penny a quart, was conveyed daily in watering-carts to indicated points in St. Helier. I did not learn whether the demand was a large one; I think that, at first, the people felt some misgiving as to whence exactly on the town beach the water was pumped into the carts, for the main drain discharges on to this beach. In any case, I was unable to discern that the effort of the States to sell the English Channel at one penny per quart had attained to anything like an overwhelming success, at any rate at first; later on, the demand increased, and in the end became difficult to satisfy.

Those who have not experienced lack of salt cannot readily imagine the sheer misery of having no salt upon the table. Salt is taken as a matter of course, until, all saltlessly, one has to eat a plate of boiled potatoes, a helping of brussels sprouts, or a dish of boiled beans, to say nothing of cabbage or cauliflower. Without salt we could hardly swallow these foods, which for so long were all that we had as hot dishes to enable us to keep body and soul together.

Then, in addition all sorts of articles, which one normally takes for granted, became unprocurable. Note-paper, envelopes and all forms of stationery, ink, pencils, glue, paper-fasteners, rubber bands, sealing-wax and pins disappeared completely.

The only premises which continued to offer some invitation to enter and buy were those of the chemists and druggists, and even here most of the bottles on the shelves were partly or wholly empty, with little or no prospect of being soon refilled. Well-known brands of proprietary articles were exhausted. A very inferior French substitute for aspirin came occasionally on sale, but not invalid foods, malt or meat extracts, cod liver oil or patent cereals of any description could be purchased without the production of a doctor's order, and not always with that.

And now a new industry made its appearance. Many of the smaller shops, and some, indeed, of the more pretentious, despairing of any possibility of laying in new stocks for years to come, opened their windows to the display of second-hand goods. In some cases sales were effected on a commission basis; in others, the goods offered had been purchased from persons eager to realise their value. Occasionally, it was the practice to sell to the highest bidder over a period of time; thus, on entering to enquire the price of a battered aluminium kettle, a much-worn pair of shoes, or an imitation pearl necklace, you would be informed: 'Our last bid was 25s. Time's up next Monday.' But usually the goods were for immediate sale, at astonishingly high prices.

By the end of the second year of the Occupation, the supply of clothing for both sexes, especially for the working classes, had already begun to assume the aspect of a first-class problem. Such clothing, by mid-September 1940, had already been rationed but, before long, ration-cards were useless, for there was nothing left to buy. By the end of that year, the Constable of St. Helier was appealing, on behalf of the poor, for women's and children's clothing, an appeal in still more urgent terms being launched in January 1941. As will be understood, however, all material had been bought up by the Germans and shipped out of the Island. The public were, therefore, implored to send all unwanted articles to a named centre to be cut up and re-made. I understand that the response was very generous, although of course, wholly insufficient for the needs of more than a fraction of the more destitute and deserving cases.

But the straits to which, in regard to shoes and footwear, the working classes were soon reduced were truly lamentable. Many of the men and women were compelled to walk long distances to their daily work; shoe-leather quickly wore out, and often there was nothing with which to effect repairs. At the end of April 1941, due to lack of leather, the soling of shoes with that material could no longer be undertaken. Shoes were, therefore 'clogged' with wood. For women, a kind of wooden-soled sandal made its appearance, the uppers being made of canvas or other stout material. Many of these contrivances, however, could only be worn with great discomfort, whilst the noise produced by their impact upon the stone pavements of the town was at first distracting; but in course of time, the public appeared to grow accustomed to the unholy clatter of unyielding soles, and in the end acceptance of this moderately successful remedy came to be general.

During the month of August 1940, the local Press gave great assistance to the public. In order to facilitate the vast amount of barter which had necessarily grown up, *The Evening Post* very thoughtfully opened an Exchange and Mart column in each daily issue. The people were thus enabled to offer goods for goods, articles for articles. A perusal of this column, had it not indicated the pathetic straits to which the islanders had been reduced, would often have appeared both interesting and amusing. There, you saw every imaginable thing offered in exchange for every conceivable *quid pro quo.* At times, the sanguine advertiser, after specifying the nature of his hopes, would offer a hostage to fortune by the addition of the two little simple words 'or what,' the intention being, should the exchange demanded not be forthcoming, to gamble

103

upon an offer of something equally or still more acceptable.

This Exchange and Mart column was in the full exercise of its very useful functions when, on June 7th, 1941, at a time when the public had grown appreciably accustomed to the convenience which it offered, the States Department of Essential Commodities issued an unnecessary and arbitrary Order which crippled it. This Order provided that, to obtain any rationed food-stuff by exchange or barter was an indictable offence. Immediately, of course, all advertisements relating to that class of goods ceased. In the following month of September, the same Department issued a second Order providing that the sale or offer to sell, or the exchange or offer to exchange, of practically every description of food, whether rationed or not, required a licence by the Food Control. To the Order was appended a list which specified no less than thirty-six articles which might not change hands, whatever quantities one might possess.

There being no possible machinery whereby this obstructive decree, as ill-advised as it was uselessly oppressive, could be enforced, the public paid not the slightest attention to it. In advertisements in the Exchange and Mart column of *The Evening Post*, the intention of the order was effectually evaded by the use of the two little words 'or what,' which, in nine cases out of ten, brought offers of all kinds of food-stuffs, both rationed and unrationed. I mention this as an example of the many consistently unhelpful orders published during the Occupation by short-sighted officials.

But the Press was unable radically to relieve the clothing shortage. By this time, all articles of clothing, as well as footwear, were changing hands at fabulous prices. Cases of housebreaking and theft, both by day and night, having for their object the abstraction of clothing of all kinds, grew in frequency; stolen clothes, in many cases, realised prices which made the risks incurred well worth while. Householders would wake in the morning to find doors or windows forced, indispensable articles of apparel missing, forcing them to beg or borrow from friends or neighbours to enable them to appear in public. In one case, an unfortunate descended to find that the whole of his stock of footwear had disappeared. He was, therefore, compelled to proceed to his business, on a rainy morning, in a pair of bedroom slippers. How he succeeded in replacing this grievous loss I never knew but the case was reported in the Press, and he received much sympathy, I hope of a practical kind.

These thefts were all part of a curious system. Among the more lasting effects of the German Occupation was the corruption of a not insignificant proportion of Jersey youth. Lack of discipline in the home produced a number of young people completely devoid of guiding principles. These youths, who at the beginning of the Occupation were still at school, were responsible for much of the lawlessness of this period. Their future is a pressing problem of great concern to all. The Occupation was particularly hard, also, on those children who would normally have concluded their education on the Mainland and who, at a most important period in their lives, were unable to leave the Island. The years passed, during which they grew from boyhood to young manhood in almost complete educational inaction, losing, through no fault of their own, most valuable time in which they should have completed their qualifying preparation for some business or profession.

The Germans, moreover, had a very bad effect on many women and young girls. At first, very naturally, the troops were regarded with repugnance, but as time passed by that feeling underwent a certain degree of modification. Probably the chief reason for this is to be found in gradual realisation of the fact that there was money to be made out of the Hun.

Soon after the arrival of the troops and the establishment in the hotels and boarding-houses of officers' and non-commissioned officers' messes, numbers of domestic servants were required and engaged at double the normal wage. A further inducement was the superiority and comparative abundance of food which they enjoyed. German officers kept excellent and well-provided tables. Then, again, instead of remaining indoors for five or six days of the week, officers' servants of both sexes were free every afternoon until six o'clock. In a short time the superiority of German employment was spread widely abroad. Men, previously perfectly satisfied with their work and wages, accepted engagements in various capacities and always at largely increased rates of pay, often leaving employers whom they had long served. About this time, the islanders began to acquire a working knowledge of the German language. Children and young people who, by order of the Civil Commandant, were now assiduously learning German in the Island schools, became extremely fluent, establishing thereby a ready and highly undesirable intimacy with the soldiers, with the result that, little by little, many among the troops succeeded in placing themselves on a footing of easy familiarity in Jersey homes.

Familiarity naturally led to immorality, a wave of which swept the Island. The result of this widespread licentiousness was a startling rise in the rate of Island illegitimacy. A terrible situation thus arose in which women, married to British serving soldiers, bore German children and registered them as the legitimate offspring of their husbands. Divorce, it should be noted, is unobtainable in Jersey!

But we have wandered away from consideration of the clothing shortage. In October 1942, the States, through the Department of Essential Commodities, proceeded to 'control' an immense list of articles of almost every conceivable description from bicycles to perambulators, from jewellery to glass and chinaware. Even pharmaceutical and toilet articles were gathered in, and, of course, clothing and footwear. This meant that those articles could only be acquired from such retailers as the States saw fit to license, and at prices fixed by the Department. That was the general impression, at any rate.

Let us now contract the sums demanded for the commoner articles of women's wear imported from France, with the pre-occupation prices. It should be clearly understood that the items included are such as would be suitable for young women of the working classes. The following table is illuminating. It should be remembered that it presents the inflated prices at their very minimum.

	Maximum Pre-War Prices	Minimum Occupation Price
Overcoats	50s.	100s.
Costumes	40s.	200s.
Raincoats	20s.	50s.
Jumpers	5s. 11d.	15s. 11d.
Stockings (artificial silk)	2s. 11d.	8s. 4d.
Socks (per pair)	1s.	4s. 3d.
Nightdresses	6s. 11d.	30s.
Shoes	8s. 11d.	25s. 6d.
Dress material (per yard)	2s. 11d.	23s.
Knitting wool (1¼ oz. ball)	9d.	4s. 3d.

Thus to knit an ordinary jumper, the cost of wool alone would exceed fifty shillings.

It will, therefore, be readily appreciated that thrifty, wage-earning women and girls were hard put to it to keep abreast of the new and inflated demands upon their modest purses. The foregoing figures have been carefully checked, and the question was constantly asked us to who chiefly benefited by these mercilessly high prices?

No satisfactory answer was forthcoming, but some little light is shed upon the matter by a Police Court case reported on April 5th, 1943. On that date, a man was charged with the theft of 2 lb. of wool, officially stated to be valued at 16s., or 8s. per pound. The price of the same wool to the public was 24s. per pound. Someone was therefore making a profit of exactly two hundred per cent.

Earthenware and glass were unobtainable. In August 1942, a States Department imported and offered for sale a small consignment of very inferior earthenware from France, suitable for kitchen use.

A serious problem in almost all households was that connected with the efficient maintenance of the *batterie de cuisine*, of the pots and pans which prepared for table the meagre fare which was all that remained to us. As the saucepan, the frying pan or the kettle developed leakages, there was no means of replacing them, for, while none of these indispensable articles was on sale, repairs, especially to aluminium vessels, were out of the question. Occasionally a battered kettle or saucepan of that metal in the last stages of decrepitude, would make its appearance in the window of a second-hand emporium, but those heaven-sent opportunities of effecting renewals were rare. To such straits were many persons reduced that, on one occasion, a somewhat self-conscious old lady was seen in the shop of a well-known retailer tentatively examining an indispensable utensil which ordinarily reposes decently concealed in the bedside cupboard, and remarking hopefully that, if she could find a lid for it, it might prove useful for boiling or stewing!

CHAPTER SIX

FURTHER HARDSHIPS

THE death-rate normally round about 12 or 13 per thousand of the population, soared, in some months to 21 and over, December 1943, when the official report returned 21·2 being a notable example. In January 1945, however, this figure was officially given at 35·6, which is statistical proof of the hardship suffered by the people of Jersey. Sudden death, due to syncope, became common; fainting fits were experienced by persons unable to account for them except on the score of long-continued malnutrition. The people grew thin, their features pinched by privation and want. Elasticity disappeared from their gait. Their clothing hung upon them. The cases of invalids and of those recovering from sickness or operation were desperate, for little or nothing could be found to assist their convalescence. It is true that, on medical certificate, the Food Control at times issued authority for the purchase of a few ounces of rice or gruel-flour, but never in sufficient quantity to produce any appreciable result.

All this is not surprising when the food position is really understood. Normal strength and vitality could just not be maintained. As we have seen, meat, sugar and fats were rationed very severely; there were neither fish nor eggs; milk was short. Eleven and a half ounces of potatoes, a proportion of which were often unfit to eat, and ten and two sevenths ounces of bread were all that remained; spread these quantities over three daily meals and they will not go far. There was often a sufficiency of garden produce; but supplies frequently failed, and even when available, provided nothing in the shape of a dish which a hungry man or woman would find either appetising or sustaining. There was a small ration of bitter, so-called breakfast meal which few could look in the face.

So difficult was it, therefore, to maintain health, that the Black Market was freely resorted to. In Britain the rations, meagre though they were, sufficed to maintain moderately good health, and resort to illegal methods of obtaining food was, no doubt rightly, regarded as scandalous and mischievous. But the growth of the Black Market in Jersey cannot be judged by the same standards.

I have no hesitation in saying that, in Jersey, the Black Market proved a boon and a blessing to large numbers of people, many of whom, I am well assured, would not be alive to-day had it not been for the additional nourishment and strength which they derived from the indispensable food whereof it was their only channel of supply.

It would no doubt be incorrect to state that, as an institution, the Black Market was openly conducted; but they were certainly few who, having the means, did not know where to apply for the needs of the moment. Practically everybody in Jersey, possessed of the necessary wherewithal, had recourse to this theoretically illicit source of supply. No effective steps whatsoever were at any time taken to check it, and I have no recollection of any offender having been proceeded against at any time.

After all, self-preservation is the first law of nature. That being so, in the circumstances in which we found ourselves, I have no word of reprobation or reproof for the man who, to maintain himself and those dearest to him in some semblance of health and well-being, avails himself, for that purpose, of all the means at his disposal. The sheer hollow insincerity of those who, while losing no opportunity of themselves laying hands upon every article of food that came their way, fulminated savagely and unceasingly at other supporters of what they hypocritically professed to regard as The Unclean Thing was sufficiently proved by the complete absence of any steps taken by them to bring it to an end. The whole fact was that, with notably few exceptions, everybody with the means at his or her command who could find a secret seller, was in it, and there

110

we may leave all further consideration of this aspect of the matter.

It may not be without interest to furnish examples of a few of the prices paid by purchasers of goods obtained in Jersey in the Black Market:

Beef, Veal or Pork	£1 7s. 10d. per lb.
Fowls	£1 5s. to £2 10s. each
Turkeys	£7 to £20 each
Rabbits	15s. to 35s. each
Butter	£3 to £5 per lb.
Sugar	15s. to 25s. per lb.
Cooking Fat	30s. to 35s. per lb.
Eggs	4s. 3d. and upwards each
Tea	£10 to £25 per lb.
Wheat (unground)	£20 to £50 per cwt.
Whisky	£7 to £10 per bottle
Tobacco (Jersey grown)	£18 to £20, finally to £50 per lb.

Fortunes were not unnaturally made with goods at these prices. Men in humble circumstances gifted with the ability and the foresight to sail with the tide speedily found themselves in independent circumstances. Some among them, indeed, blossomed into property owners on a considerable scale for, of course, the purchase of real estate formed the only means of investment open to them. Some of these men were Jersey Fagins who employed youths and young men to steal provisions and other goods for them which they sold in the Black Market. In one case two youths, doubtless incited thereto, broke into the States Food Control Store at night and drove away the Department's motor-van laden with cases of brandy, whisky, and quantities of tinned provisions valued at a large sum. In this case, however, fortune did not favour the brave; they and their instigator were promptly discovered and arrested; in due course they paid the penalty for the delinquency. I remember that, in the course of the Police Court evidence, one of the youths, a boy of about 16 years of age, was stated already to have a balance at the bank of something like £800. Though young, he must have been fairly old at the game.

Petrol was also sold in the Black Market. By the Summer of 1940, owing to the fact that stocks had been requisitioned by the Germans, leaving little if any for the civil population, medical practitioners were compelled to inform the public that they could no longer attend confinements in private houses. Expectant mothers, therefore, were notified that they must make arrangements for admission to the General Hospital, the Dispensary, or to one or other of the several nursing homes, established in St. Helier. Occasionally, medical men were enabled to supply themselves with small quantities of petrol in the Black Market; but the general lack gave rise to much inconvenience both in the cases of doctors and their patients. As time went on and their motor-cars were taken from them, medical practitioners riding bicycles did their utmost to attend to their patients, often in circumstances of great difficulty and no little danger, for ill-health was increasing.

Tuberculosis, not previously unduly widespread, became common. Due to lack of fat in the people's diet, rheumatoid and arthritic maladies increased and multiplied. Diptheria assumed epidemic form; jaundice was severe. Recuperative resiliency lacking, maladies of the throat and chest became persistent and difficult to throw off, and long continued recourse to nourishment of an inferior or unsuitable character reacted disastrously upon the function of the alimentary canal.

During 1942 and thereafter, cases of suicide and attempted suicide were reported with depressingly increasing frequency, as loss of stamina, the wane of vitality and final desperation drew many of the weaker minded to the Nirvana offered by the gas oven.

That convenient avenue of escape, however, was cut off on September 11th, 1944, when the supply of gas, both for lighting and cooking, came to an end. There was no more coal and no prospect of obtaining further supplies.

About this time stocks of drugs and remedies of all kinds were running perilously low. Supplies in the possession of chemists, it was estimated, would last for no longer than six weeks. Anaesthetics, it was reported, would be no longer obtainable after the end of October. Thereafter, it was greatly feared surgeons would be compelled to operate in the appalling conditions which prevailed in pre-anaesthetic days. Even for skin diseases and other maladies requiring them, there were no longer any ointments available.

Everything was short. As we have seen, the waning Summer of 1944 brought thousands of German troops, their escape cut off by the loss of the French ports, into the Island. The havoc, already referred to, caused by the sudden increase in the population, was not restricted to food.

But that was not all. By the end of August, it was perfectly evident that, unless relief came speedily, the coming Winter would bring with it a degree of suffering such as few could have foreseen or anticipated. In a memorandum addressed in that month to the Occupying Authority, the Bailiff pointed out that after the month of September no coal, coal-dust or coke would be available for household heating or cooking (gas, it will be remembered came to an end on the 11th of that month). It was moreover shown that only 1,600 of the 3,490 tons of wood regarded as a minimum quantity for providing one hot meal a day in each household, could be obtained. Even this was dependent on transport facilities, weather conditions and other considerations.

To cope, in some degree, with this disastrous situation, the States arranged, for the benefit of workers and the poor, that oven accommodation to undertake the cooking of one hot meal a day should be made available. For this purpose, I believe, a number of additional ovens were built, and some relief was experienced; those availing themselves of the facility providing the food in suitable vessels. Communal kitchens, soup distributing centres and people's registered restaurants were also set on foot. These went some way to provide more or less hot food for the working classes and the poor.

According to the Bailiff's memorandum to the German Platzkommandant, the arrangements for cooking one hot meal a day were widely accepted and adopted. About 6,500 households registered for this facility, while, in addition, the communal kitchen provided highly appreciated meals for 1,400 persons.

Unhappily, oven cooking failed at first to provide a complete remedy for the lack of household fires. At the beginning, owing to insufficient completely dry wood fuel, the necessary degree of heat in the ovens could not at times be obtained or maintained. Persons who carried their mid-day meals to be cooked in the morning, found, on calling for them that certain vegetables such as potatoes, parsnips and carrots were still hard. Arrived, therefore, at their chilly, fireless homes, working men, after five hours of hard, breakfastless toil, found awaiting them a mass of luke-warm, half-cooked vegetables, swimming in rapidly cooling water, with a slice of dry bread, and with no salt to help it down. This constituted the promised one hot meal of the day.

By this time, there was no longer any butter ration. A so-called reserve of some eighteen or twenty tons of butter which had been deposited over a long period in the States refrigerator, was suddenly requisitioned by the German Authorities, and handed over.

Butter, as everybody knows, is a most valuable food, containing a high degree of nutrition. The public had learned from the Bailiff's memorandum to the Platzkommandant already mentioned, that issues of butter would continue up to December 31st, but he had counted without the Germans.

Next in importance to the grave food question, came that of winter lighting. Early in the autumn, it became known that, through the exhaustion of oil and coal, electricity would cease at the end of the year. The unfortunate islanders, by that time in a condition approaching real starvation, would therefore find themselves with no light after sunset, and no heating facilities whatsoever beyond a small allowance of wood fuel scarcely sufficient to boil the saucepan containing their meagre breakfast meal.

The future seemed to hold but little worth living for, yet the people went about their daily concerns with a cheerful, apparently care-free, if noticeably emaciated, appearance. It was easy to get a smile from them. They were not downhearted.

114

One and all, with very few exceptions, were perfectly sure that it 'would be all over soon.' I have often thought that, in the darkly ominous outlook of the Autumn of 1944, the people were more sustained by hope than by their starvation fare.

The States Authorities, on the other hand, were less sanguine. In the memorandum issued by the Bailiff to the German command in the month of August, the following recapitulation was appended. It made the near future look bleak.

Butter, 2 oz. weekly ration. Sufficient to last to December 31st.

Sugar, 3 oz. weekly ration. Sufficient to last to November 18th.

Salt, for bakers only. Sufficient to last to November 30th.

Macaroni. Sufficient to last to November 15th.

Dried Beans. 3 rations of 7 oz. remaining.

Cheese. 4 oz. ration. Sufficient to last until October 15th.

Tinned vegetables. One ration remaining in stock.

Tinned fish. One ration remaining in stock.

Tinned milk. One ration remaining in stock.

Matches. One ration of four boxes per household remaining in stock.

Dripping. Not enough for one ration.

Oil (Cooking). Enough for one ration of under half-pint remaining.

Saccharine. Enough for two rations of 100 tabloids remaining.

Soap. None.

The Authorities decided that, as the public had been drastically rationed for over four years, it was undesirable to prolong the duration of the stocks of goods remaining by further reducing rations.

A novel but unenviable experience was foreshadowed by the approaching complete exhaustion of the match supply. To be entirely destitute of means of lighting the kitchen or drawing-room fire, a candle, which probably cost twenty shillings in any case, a lamp or a cigarette, is a hardship easily appreciated, more especially in the depth of Winter. Nevertheless, Jersey finally went matchless.

In the long, apparently unending period of our anxiety and want, we often wondered if any thought of our sufferings, both mental and physical, ever occurred to those Statesmen in London to whom we felt we had some right to look for the means to keep body and soul together. We had heard over the wireless sympathetic references in Parliament to our unhappy lot, and hope expressed that our unenviable plight would not be duly prolonged. Thereafter, for many months, we heard nothing more. Some there were who clung to the heartening belief that, sooner or later, Britain would come to our assistance; but, as time went on and nothing happened, and as an endless vista of future months—perhaps years—of monotonous misery stretched out before us, even the most sanguine became overshadowed by a lowering cloud of doubt growing daily darker.

We had been left, it seemed, by London, to the tender mercies of the Germanic hordes. The belief, and it was a bitter one, gained ground and became widespread that His Majesty's Government had either forgotten or, preoccupied by considerations of greater importance, had left us to our fate. In the long, bleak years through which we passed, we asked each other openly and frequently whether Britain had really lost sight of some 50,000 Britishers in the Channel Islands, dragging out their weary days in misery and hunger only about a hundred miles from the Mainland coast. That was what it looked like. From time to time we heard over the wireless when, with tightened belts, we were gloomily speculating upon what form the next cut in our meagre rations would take, statements of the thousands of tons of food exported by the Allied Governments to Greece, to Italy, to Russia; not unnaturally we wondered why not to Jersey. Perhaps this was unavoidable; but it should not be wondered at if many felt bitter; all they got from the Government were empty words—never a grain of hope.

As Christmas 1944 approached, rumour spread wild assurances of apparently mythical aid said to be coming through the

116

instrumentality of the International Red Cross, from 'A Protecting Power.' Many assured each other, with a stern *visage de circonstance*, that they had undeniable information that ships laden with all possible requirements were daily expected from Sweden. A policeman patrolling the wharf, it was said, had heard orders issued to pilots to stand by and hold themselves in readiness to bring the vessels into port. It was reported that the Bailiff was in wireless communication with Geneva, and that, Switzerland being our Protecting Power, parcels containing luxuries to which we had long been strangers were expected daily by *air*! The German Authorities, it was whispered, had signified their willingness to allow ships from the United States to transport food, clothing and coal to the Channel Islands and safe conducts had already been transmitted through Spain, to Washington. These were but a few of the amazing stories to which the famine-stricken Jersey people lent a willing if doubtful ear.

But nothing came; and day by day the future grew darker and more menacing.

Little by little hope died away, and we went home to our daily meals of a little boiled potato, a little cabbage, a few beans, and a piece of dry bread. For a long period, too, we received, every fourteen days, our dole of four ounces of poor-quality meat with bone, but this went nowhere.

On November 22nd, through the dark grey murk of a typical November morning, came our first apparent real ray of light. At the beginning it was only a rumour; but, as the day advanced, it spread and gained each hour in dubious detail and circumstantial volume. A reply had at least been received from our Protecting Power.

Help was coming. It was on the way. It might reach us any day. We were to receive parcels. There was to be a parcel for everybody. We were to have not only food but soap. Great was our joy; but almost equally great was our scepticism and unbelief.

But, in the later afternoon, all doubt was set at rest. *The Evening Post* contained, in German and English, the following pregnant message:

'NOTICE. As a result of negotiations instigated [sic] by the Occupying Authorities re supplies for the civilian population, a delivery of medical supplies, soap and food parcels has been promised as a first measure.

(Signed) Der Befehlshaber des Kalaninseln.'

So, at long last, we had something to look forward to. It was still rather less than five weeks to Christmas; but much might happen in that time. That night, that amazing twenty-second of November, life assumed a rosier aspect. Our evening meal, of luke-warm, saltless mashed potatoes, or other vegetable matter was viewed with slightly more disfavour than usual as, in anticipation, we were already feverishly opening those life-saving parcels. Fancy rioted with the fascinating problem of what they were likely to contain, and the hopeful views of prospective recipients varied with age, sex and desire. Many were the excited discussions, countless were the prophetic arguments. Finally, we all went to bed to dream of string and brown paper shrouding from our eager view all sorts of long undreamed-of luxuries from tea to coffee, from chocolate to cigarettes.

But the days passed. They became weeks, but no ship was sighted, no parcels arrived either by sea or air. People began to realise that though for a time life had been full of promise, that promise bore nothing in the shape of a contract stamp. Optimists felt gloomily that, after all, optimism was but a species of wistfulness which, in nine cases out of ten, turned gradually sour. Hope became doubt; doubt ended in despondency. To mention the word parcels was to court derision not unmingled with profanity. People began to say that the whole thing was neither more nor less than a gigantic leg-pull.

November 1944, saw the bread ration for everybody, adults, workers and adolescents alike, cut down to four and a quarter pounds per week, or nine and a half ounces per day. We were further informed that one milkless day per week would begin on December 11th. By this time, we had no longer any sugar, any butter or any salt. How manual labourers could work at all on such rations was a mystery. They grew more and more

118

emaciated. Many of them, in their worn-out clothing and broken, ruinous footwear, stalked feebly in the darkness of the winter mornings to their daily toil. It was terribly saddening to think of their nightly return to cheerless, lightless, fireless homes, only to find there scarcely sufficient tasteless food to keep them alive.

The first reaction of the Germans to the report that provisions might be expected for the civil population took the form of an intensive search of all farms in the Island for wheat, oats and potatoes. Obviously, they reasoned somewhat as follows: 'Well, if civilians are going to be fed from outside, we can now squeeze them for all the foodstuffs that we can possibly get out of them. So why should we go hungry?'

Every farm building was accordingly subjected to a rigorous examination. Leaving a small and in many cases wholly insufficient quantity of the necessaries referred to for the family's needs during the approaching winter, squads of non-commissioned officers and men noted down the remainder which, blocked for the moment from sale or barter, was in due course removed for German use against a small payment. Even the oat rations for horses officially authorised by the Department of Agriculture and the seed potatoes for spring planting were commandeered. As Christmas approached, poultry in farms and civilian possession were counted and numbers noted.

The natural uneasiness aroused by the poultry census resulted in farmers and other owners taking steps to safeguard their birds. Some promptly killed and sold them, others sent them into hiding or other safe keeping. Apprised of this, the Germans published a soothing notice stating that the count was 'simply meant to find out the total number of poultry in the Island.' Notice was given that any rumours that poultry were to be confiscated were quite without foundation. This, of course, was intended to reassure owners and to discourage them from concealing or otherwise disposing of their birds, thus facilitating their seizure for, immediately afterwards, at a farm known to me, twenty-six fowls were arbitrarily seized and carried off, leaving only six for the unfortunate farmer, whose indignant protests were received with contemptuous laughter.

For the consumption of the German troops at Christmas, it was estimated that, in spite of the reassuring notice mentioned above, upwards of 3,000 head of poultry were carried off.

In mid-December, evidently suspecting that sooner or later Red Cross officials might arrive in Jersey and ask awkward questions, the German Authorities published a notice furnishing a list of centres in the country districts where military police would be stationed for the purpose of checking nightly robberies. But, as cases had been known where, on being summoned, these men had enthusiastically joined the marauders and shared the loot, the notice fell some distance short of either inspiring confidence or dispelling apprehension.

But, if Christmas 1944, brought nothing else, it brought at long last, definite assurances that help was coming. Official statements were published to the effect that a Swedish steamer would sail from Lisbon with medical necessaries, provisions and soap for the Channel Islands and that she would arrive about Christmas time. In the light of previous disappointment, nobody believed it; but this time the statement appeared to be well founded for, late in December, the news reached us that the ship had actually reached Guernsey.

The arrival of the vessel in the sister island failed to arouse much enthusiasm. It provided a doubtful topic of conversation, but it was only when the Bailiff of Jersey left on a small patrol boat for St. Peter Port that it was finally realised that the long-promised help might at last be at hand. What was taking the Bailiff to Guernsey nobody seemed to know. As he did not return on board the Swedish ship, but was carefully shepherded back in the German patrol boat, it seemed doubtful if he had been allowed, except in the presence of German witnesses, to establish contact with the Red Cross officials who accompanied that vessel. Colour was lent to the supposition, moreover, by the elaborate precautions taken by the German Authorities, on the arrival of the ship in Jersey, to prevent any civilian from communication with her, or any contact between the crew and the shore. During the vessel's stay in St. Helier, from December 31st to January 4th, the entire port was surrounded by armed German guards and sentries, with orders to allow no person to approach or leave the ship. The working of the cargo was undertaken exclusively by German naval ratings, the only civilians engaged upon it being the electric-crane men who were also kept under close surveillance. As the cases were landed, they were at once loaded upon lorries and carts and driven away, escorted by armed soldiers and members of the St John Ambulance, to a large warehouse which had been specially set apart for their reception.

All these precautions were clearly due to a feeling of nervous fear lest the brutal and illegal procedure of the German Authorities in the Island, and the many abuses which they had committed, should leak out if members of the civilian population found opportunity of establishing contact with members of the Swedish ship's company.

The immediate help which reached us took the form of parcels, the gift of the Canadian Red Cross, the New Zealand Red Cross and the British Red Cross, which despatched a number of special parcels for invalids. In addition, shipments of salt and medical necessaries reached us, together with a small quantity of tobacco and cigarettes, a kindly present from the Dominion of New Zealand. Unfortunately, however, no soap was included in the parcels.

Special appreciation was felt for a number of layettes, the personal gift of Lady Campbell, the wife of the British Ambassador to Portugal. The kind thought which inspired this unexpected example of womanly sympathy at once struck the popular imagination, and though she may never hear of it, the gratitude of many totally unprovided mothers was as real as it was heart-felt.

'It was intimated that, in so far as might be found possible, further supplies in the form of parcels would be despatched to Jersey monthly. This was a disappointment; for we had been led to hope that, as in the case of prisoners of war and interned persons in Germany, supplies might reach us every fortnight. Still, we were grateful; a fund was immediately started to furnish to the International Red Cross a practical proof of our whole-hearted gratitude, which was just a little damped when

121

the Department of Essential Commodities cancelled the week's meat ration.

The Island of Jersey Red Cross Fund was well supported. The lists of subscriptions for the first seven days totalled between £8,000 and £9,000, the amount finally reached exceeding £130,000. The officials of the International Red Cross, on their next arrival in Jersey, were greatly gratified at the magnitude and heartiness of the response made.

The Red Cross Commissioners who accompanied the ship were fairly informed of the sorry plight in which the islanders had for so long existed. Having carefully examined the general situation in both the Islands, and received detailed particulars, they are said to have expressed horror and astonishment at the facts disclosed, together with keen eagerness to make all necessary representations with a view to ensuring early and regular relief.

Among the various proposals tentatively accepted by them were a monthly delivery of a shipment of flour sufficient to provide each adult, if possible, with a weekly ration of 6 lb. of bread in place of the 4¼ lb. so long issued; and an allocation of candles, matches, yeast, leather, boot-repairing equipment and vegetable seeds. The Commissioners recognised that the provision of fuel was a necessity of an importance equal to that of uncooked food-stuffs. For this purpose, gas coal was considered the best solution since, in addition to gas for cooking purposes, the resulting gas coke would provide a valuable fuel for the heating of dwelling houses and institutions. Curiously enough, no mention appears to have been made of the need for lamp-oil, so that, to all appearance, the people would continue indefinitely without any means of domestic lighting.

On January 4th, 5th and 6th, 1945, the parcels were finally delivered. I understand that the distribution was effected with smoothness and despatch and reflected great credit upon the many tradesmen, farmers and others to whose well-directed voluntary efforts this was due.

No sooner were the Islanders in possession of this Red Cross assistance than the German Authorities published an Order laying down that, in view of the arrival of comestible help for the civil population, all persons having in their possession small stated quantities of stored provisions, must proceed to distribute any surplus over and above such quantities among their less fortunate neighbours before the 15th of the month. Any excess amounts found in private houses after that date, it was intimated, would be confiscated.

The object underlying this Order was sufficiently plain. It was simply to furnish the German Kommandantur with a pretext for entering and searching occupied premises, less with the object of discovering concealed hoards of provisions, than for the purpose of systematically hunting for wireless receiving sets, cameras, or indeed any stray articles which might arouse the cupidity of the soldiers entrusted with the task. If, of course, they succeeded in unearthing hidden stores of food, so much the better for them.

About the same time, a further Order made its appearance directing that, with a view further to conserve the dwindling food reserves, no household might keep more than one dog. In cases where two or more were kept the additional animals were to be killed immediately.

From January 13th, three milkless days in each week were announced. We therefore appreciated most gratefully the large tins of dried milk which our Red Cross parcels-contained. It appeared that since, the civil population had received small supplies of butter from overseas, our Island milk was required for making butter for the Germans, who now claimed the whole of the butter produced in the Island.

On the same date we finally lost the use of our telephones. The supply of electric current, soon to come to an end, was so restricted that the weekly allowance for lighting was now reduced to one kilowatt (unit) per house per week. This meant limitation to the use of one low-powered bulb for about an hour a night, current being finally cut off at 10.30 p.m. More fortunate were the few who possessed some kind of oil-lamp and a small supply of paraffin.

And now came a particularly brutal German order. I have described elsewhere the miseries which resulted from almost complete lack of fuel.

On January 16th, the Platzkommandant, with immediate effect, published an Order prohibiting the collection, cutting, or gathering of any description of wood for fuel, even by owners or occupiers of land, in private gardens, farms, public parks or roads. Any person found so cutting or gathering wood became liable to severe punishment, while tools employed for the purpose were to be confiscated. To give effect to the Orders the troops were authorised, in cases of non-observance, to seize wood collected and impound implements used.

This savage, gratuitous barbarity, aimed as it was, at the poorest and most privation-stricken of the population, aroused deep and most natural resentment. It was not much that the cold, misery-haunted, half-starved people asked; only a little indulgence to enable them, by their own exertions, to collect a scrap of fuel to give them a few hours' warmth in that bitter January.

But what added bitterness to bitterness, was the spectacle, all over the Island, of German troops, armed with axes and cross-cut saws, busily engaged, day after day, in cutting down and carting away well-grown trees for their own use, while the shivering islanders, to whom these trees properly belonged, were callously debarred, by formal order, from gathering up as much as an armful of the twigs that had fallen from them.

On January 25th, we bade a long farewell to our electric light. At one generating station, it was stated, there remained no more coal, while at the other exhaustion of diesel oil was given for the cause of the stoppage. That the diesel oil, which for some months had been used for supplementary lighting, should have run out surprised no one. The Black Market, too, wasted much oil. I myself received and rejected an offer of one gallon of this unusual form of lamp-oil for the modest sum of fifty Reichsmarks (£5 6s. 10d.). In all these circumstances, and with so many leakages, it was not surprising that the Power Station was compelled to close down.

But there must have been a good deal more oil than the people were led to suppose, for the Germans expressed their intention, for the purpose of working their heavy guns, of keeping the Station running. On this intelligence reaching the staff, the men, I was informed, at once unanimously notified the management that they would refuse to work for the Germans, and were prepared to quit their employment rather than do so. I believe that the Station was finally taken over by German electricians. The British staff were found other work by the Company.

Jersey remained without any kind of household lighting, and little conception can be formed, by those who have not experienced it, of the inconveniences and even hardship entailed. It should be remembered that literally thousands of persons possessed no means of artificial lighting whatsoever. Paraffin was unobtainable; candles were costly. Hundreds of houses, in temperatures which fell at times to several degrees below freezing point during the Winter, had no fires and no fuel with which to make them. In many a small household there were no matches. The Red Cross parcels did not last long; their contents were all too soon exhausted. There was only one place, after a long day of toil and a scanty cheerless evening meal of dry bread and cold vegetables, where warmth and oblivion might perchance be obtained, and that was bed. Even in bed, however, people had too much to worry about to be happy. How long would their dwindling strength stand up to daily work? What of their hard-toiling wives, whose vitality was rapidly declining? What of their emaciated, always-hungry children, clamouring for the food which it was beyond their power to provide? How long would there be work for them to do, and then what?

At the end of January the Press published some striking figures, from the office of the St. Helier Registrar. These showed that, in the small township, during that fatal month of almost continuous frost and snow, seventy-eight persons passed away, the highest number recorded since, fifteen years before, a terrible epidemic of influenza had raged. These seventy-eight deaths, unquestionably brought about by the prevailing conditions, included a large proportion of aged people cut off by want and privation. Other cases were those of persons, either young or in the prime of life, who, through sudden heart failure produced by under-nourished exhaustion, passed away at their work, while walking in the street, or were found dead in their beds in the morning.

By now the German troops, in spite of their nightly forays in search of potatoes or root-crops, were beginning to display unmistakable symptoms of the effects of protracted hunger. Their formerly tight-fitting tunics, it was observable, had commenced to sag; their faces had become thin and pinched, their cheek-bones more prominent, cheeks and eyes sunken, their general expression nervy and care-worn. To such straits were they reduced that some had actually been seen rummaging in the refuse bins awaiting collection by the municipal carts. Others openly confessed that they had supplemented their daily rations by eating limpets taken from the rocks, and the flesh of dogs and cats.

Food, for Germans and civilians alike, was now running perilously short. I have already referred to the readiness displayed by the Red Cross officials to lend a sympathetic ear to the pitiable recital of the Island's needs; but they could, of course, do no more than undertake to forward representations to the proper quarter. In the meantime, stocks of food, to which the parcels just received, however acceptable, could afford little or nothing in the way of substantial supplementation, were speedily exhausted. On the last day of January, there only remained in the hands of the States Authorities sufficient flour for ten days bread ration, while no advices had been received that any consignment was on the way or, indeed, that any supplies were about to be shipped from Lisbon.

It will be remembered that by far the greater part of the very good recent harvest had been bluntly and unceremoniously commandeered by the German Authorities for the use of the troops in occupation, while many hundreds of tons had been similarly demanded for those garrisoning the Island of Guernsey.

As January drew to its close the States Authorities found to their consternation that the people of the Island, who depended upon them for their daily bread, were now faced with sheer starvation. Hasty application was thereupon made to the German Platzkommandant for the loan of sufficient of our own wheat flour to tide us over the period pending the arrival of supplies from overseas.

This application, reasonable enough in all conscience, was curtly refused unless guarantees were furnished that flour for Jersey had been despatched and was actually *en route*— guarantees which obviously the States Authorities were in no position to give. Upon this the Bailiff requested the doubtless exultant Platzkommandant's permission to despatch a pressing message to our Protecting Power representing the urgency of the situation and soliciting an immediate reassuring reply, a message which, needless to say, should have been transmitted many weeks earlier.

Days passed, days of intense anxiety. Why a month all but a few days should have been allowed to elapse before decisive steps were taken to ascertain what measure of relief might be relied upon, it is difficult to imagine; but the fact remains that invaluable time was carelessly frittered away and wasted until ten days only remained between the islanders and stark famine in its most unbearable form, the complete lack of their daily bread.

On February 3rd, an official notice was published by the States Authorities in the following terms:

SUPERIOR COUNCIL—BREAD RATIONING

NOTICE IS HEREBY GIVEN, That in compliance with an Order of the Military Commander of the Channel Islands, bread rations will, with effect from Monday next, February 5th, be reduced to the following amounts:

> Infants, 1 lb. per week
> Children, 1 lb. 8 oz. per week
> Invalids, 1 lb. 8 oz. per week
> All other categories, 2 lb. per week

The Public is informed that the supplies of flour under the control of the States would have been sufficient to maintain the bread ration at the old scale only up to

February 10th, 1945. The reduction now ordered will, it is hoped, make possible the issue of a bread ration (on the reduced scale) up to February 17th, 1945.

On February 6th, another message from the Bailiff dealing with the situation was published in the columns of *The Evening Post*.

In that remarkable document the public were informed that *it was not until after Christmas* that any information relative to the Island's rapidly dwindling stock of flour had been conveyed to the International Red Cross. The message did not explain why the Protecting Power had not been informed of the impending danger of famine in Jersey as soon as the Germans had taken possession of the greater part of the 1944 wheat crop. The Jersey Authorities must have known, or should have known, months before Christmas, that the reduced stocks in the States' granaries could not by any possibility suffice for more than a few weeks beyond the end of the year, and yet they would appear to have made no attempt whatsoever to communicate the people's growing danger to the only possible source of help. The Bailiff's message calmly proceeded as follows:

'The proposed cut (to 2 lb. of bread per week) should make possible a continuation of the Bread Ration for a week after February 10th.

'If help does not reach us by then, either by actual arrival of flour or by the promise of future supplies, the Bread Ration must cease completely.'

On Tuesday, February 14th, the chartered Red Cross steamer *Vega* arrived with more parcels from Lisbon. Hope that she might be conveying the necessary flour to supply the hungry islanders with bread was promptly dispelled by another message from the Bailiff. Published the following day, this brief communication, in a quotation from a letter stated to have been received from the Red Cross Commissioner in the Portuguese capital, informed an anxiously expectant public that, although flour was available in Lisbon, the British Red Cross Society in London had decided, despite representations of the extreme urgency of the case, that its shipment should be deferred until the vessel's next voyage to Jersey. Hope was expressed that the consequences of the delay might not be serious.

The comfort conveyed by this letter, which was stated to have been despatched to the Bailiff, was decidedly cold. It appeared to mean that, for several weeks at least, due to an alleged decision of the Red Cross Authorities in London, Jersey would receive no flour for its daily loaf. Another instalment of parcels which the steamship *Vega* transported was received with some coolness. It was bread that the people wanted; not chocolate or jam.

Quite unexpectedly, a one-pound loaf was distributed on February 23rd, by the Food Control. It was evident, however, that no more would be forthcoming until the arrival of flour from Lisbon. Indeed, this was the only bread ration from February 17th, until March 12th, when flour at last arrived.

On April 17th, a notice published in *The Evening Post* stated that, for the following week, the ration of five pounds of potatoes per head of the civil population would be reduced to one pound, and that thereafter the issue of potato rations would be indefinitely suspended.

In spite, therefore, of International Red Cross parcels, received at intervals of about three weeks, the future food supply appeared to be almost if not quite as uncertain as ever, for no care or management could possibly enable the use of parcels to extend over twenty-one days. In the case of nine-tenths of the population, indeed, it would be safe to say that the contents of their parcels were completely exhausted in less than one-third of that period.

Yet even this was but the prelude to worse hardship. On April 19th, a Food Delegation published a notice stating that, on and after the 23rd of the month, a number of the ovens in the urban and rural districts would close down for lack of fuel, and that the Community Restaurant and Communal Kitchen would discontinue the service of mid-day meals, which for eight months had done much excellent work and had been the main dinner centres of many hundreds of the poorer classes of the people.

Accordingly, on the date stated, eleven ovens ceased all further operation. Persons who had had recourse to them were recommended to 'contact' other bakers.

There was admittedly a lack of fuel; but it has been conservatively estimated that, of almost every tree cut down by men of the Department concerned, little more than one-third ever reached the log-cutting centres. The remainder was said to be appropriated, sold or exchanged for butter, tobacco or other farm produce otherwise unobtainable.

So, instead of going into the ovens, the fuel probably went into the Black Market. It was difficult to understand why the States took no firm action in this matter.

About the end of April, the civil population of Jersey received another blow. Though they did not know it, it was destined to be the final one. Up to that time, with three and sometimes four milkless days in each week, the people had been receiving half-a-pint of milk on each of the remaining three or four. The Germans, who were said to be consuming 18,000 quarts per week, suddenly demanded that their quantity should be practically doubled, leaving of course, little or none for the civil population. Of what representations were made to the German Commandant by the States Authorities I have naturally no knowledge. If any were made, they evidently left the former profoundly unimpressed for, on April 23rd, a notice signed by the Festungskommandant and published in *The Evening Post* was in the following terms:

1. With immediate effect it is hereby ordered that all farmers and cow-keepers must deliver, without reserve, the whole of the milk produced by their cows. Deliveries will be controlled by the Inspector of the Forces and the States.

2. Farmers and cow-keepers who commit an infraction of this Order will have their cows and grasslands confiscated, without compensation, and be punished by fine or imprisonment.

On the same day a States Department circular was issued to farmers stating that the Occupying Authority had demanded a large increase in the supply of milk, threatening, if such demand were not complied with, to slaughter 750 head of cattle per month, use military measures to obtain the milk demanded, and take control of distribution.

But deliverance was nearer than we knew. The Germans had no time to carry their Order into effect. Nemesis was at hand.

CHAPTER SEVEN

HOW THE END CAME

As 1944 drew to a close it became increasingly evident that a strong under-current of discontent existed among the troops occupying Jersey. This was due to the unfavourable character of the war *communiqués* which, despite all precautions, were leaking out and reaching the rank and file; to the harrowing contents of their letters from Germany; to the appallingly restricted rations issued to them; to the knowledge that their officers were faring far more sumptuously than they; to the devitalising monotony of their daily existence on a small island where, cut off from participation in the excitement of the conflict raging so comparatively near, many felt keenly that they were doing no good; and, finally, to extremely unpopular changes in the command of the Channel Islands.

The men carried out their drills and exercises both by day and by night. To keep them employed, they were set to digging trenches, sniping posts and bomb-proof shelters; they furnished countless fatigue-parties for tree-felling, log-cutting and the transport, in hand-carts, of the resultant fuel; they ploughed and cultivated farm-land, taken over for the planting of commandeered seed potatoes, and, one day in each week, they were exercised at the guns.

No longer did the Island people hear the raucous bellow of German marching songs. There was little song left in the troops. Displaying clear and evident signs of malnutrition and depression, completely devoid of animation, their uniforms patched and dirty, they slouched along, often out of step, with no longer any trace of their former military smartness. Others lounged about the streets and roads.

As any soldier will at once perceive, the situation in which the German troops in occupation of Jersey now found themselves was one which induced, perhaps insensibly at first, a condition of mind and body all too favourable to the reception of ideas of a character in the highest degree prejudicial to good order, military discipline and the safety of their officers, for whom they had begun to display but little regard. They had been left too long with nothing of interest to do and much to brood upon. Gradually but surely brooding gave rise to discontent; discontent, fomented doubtless by secret, provocative whispering, produced, in its turn, a state of mind ripe for some form of revolt. Thereafter anything might happen.

As the Summer of 1944 waned and passed into Autumn, rumours were heard that all was not well in the ranks of the German Army of Occupation. Small slips of extremely thin tissue-paper, covertly passed in match-boxes and in cigarette-paper covers from hand to hand, contained direct incitement to mutiny, to murder their officers, to deliver up the Island to the Allies, and to surrender. Several of these slips came into my possession and, translated, left no doubt upon my mind of the latent spirit of revolt seething in the minds of a certain section, at any rate, of the occupying Force. It is almost needless to say that, having acquainted myself of their contents, I lost no time in ridding myself of this highly dangerous matter which, brought to light in a search of my premises liable at any moment to occur, would unquestionably have placed me in a position of the gravest danger.

But nothing happened, owing to the fact, I can only suppose, that the movement had failed to attract sufficient support. So several months passed, and nothing more was heard of the matter. Late in the month of February 1945, however, another slip of paper was secretly circulated. This was of a much more decided and subversive character, its translation running as follows:

'The Russians are on the doorstep of Berlin. The Anglo-Americans stand on German soil in the West and daily their planes lay more and more German towns in ruins, daily kill

133

more of our women and children. Why?

'Hitler wanted to conquer the world. Hitler began this war. He wanted to pulverise English towns. He wanted to exterminate whole populations. The entire guilt of this insane visionary and his accomplices has been avenged. Even the most unintelligent begins by degrees to see that all Hitler's promises were nothing but pie-crust. We have only him and his Nazi clique to thank for the immeasurable sorrow that has been cast over the whole world, and above all, over the German people.

'Soldiers in Jersey. How long do you intend to take part in this, the biggest deception of all time? How long do you want to stay here and starve? The war is lost. We can do nothing to alter our common fate. On the contrary, through stubborn holding out we are spoiling our last chances of an assured future. We call upon you to surrender. Raise your voices with us against the helpless officer clique and their accomplices. A large part of the garrison is preparing for insurrection against its tormentors. Help us too and be watchful. The day approaches when you will be advised that not all Germans are blind to their fate. Set a good example and our future will be assured. Stop this tomfoolery. Organise yourselves thoroughly. You will not be alone. An experienced officer is on our side. Here in Jersey it will be settled and indeed completely. With that, you can escape the Nazi mob. Keep quiet. Await further news. Do away with Nazism, and then Germany will be a free country.'

About this time, for reasons which have never been made known, important changes took place in the command of the Channel Islands. The General Officer Commanding in Chief, Major General Count von Schmettow, who had held the position for several years, was suddenly superseded by Vice Admiral Hueffmeier, while General Wolff, stated to be a Brown-shirt, a rabid Nazi and a stern disciplinarian, and believed to have been withdrawn from the defence of Breslau where the Russians were extremely anxious to lay hands upon him, was sent to Jersey to command the troops in that Island.

The appointment of the latter officer and certain oppressive orders which he immediately issued had the effect of exacerbating prevailing discontent; intense irritation, moreover, was felt at the appointment to the Supreme Command of a Naval officer. Murmuring in the ranks grew and increased; one heard, indeed, of acts of deliberate sabotage and disregard of orders, which, if true, clearly indicated a dangerous spirit among the rank and file. What steps, if any, were taken in the matter, I had, of course, no means of knowing, but it did not appear that the measures adopted were either very firm or very efficacious.

On the morning of March 7th, shortly before noon, the town of St. Helier and the surrounding districts were shaken by a violent explosion. This explosion almost completely destroyed the Palace Hotel, the most popular hotel in the Island. The large building occupied a commanding position overlooking the south coast of the Island, and was exceedingly comfortable and well managed. On the arrival of the Germans, it was promptly taken over by them for the exclusive use of officers.

On the morning of the occurrence, which appeared to have been accurately timed, the Palace Hotel was the scene of an important conference of officers who, it afterwards transpired, were in the midst of their deliberations when the blow fell. Exactly how many persons were killed was never disclosed by the High Command, who attempted to attribute the disaster to accident; but the intelligence afterwards leaked out that about twenty-four officers were killed, and the explosion was caused by a time-bomb, an explanation which received support from the fact that one of the hotel servants was urgently warned by a friend, who was aware of the plot, not to go to work on that morning. The explosion was succeeded by fire, and only the four walls of what had so recently been a fine hotel now remain.

On the same morning an attempt was made to fire a large petrol dump situated in the eastern portion of the town This, however, failed, probably owing to hasty and imperfect organisation.

135

The effect upon the High Command of these two suggestive simultaneous occurrences must have been alarming. All pretence that either was the result of an accident had to be abandoned, for, in any case, nobody believed it. Such a pretence would in all probability have never been attempted had another slip of paper, issued by the malcontents under date March 16th, come into the possession of Headquarters. A translation of this surprising incitement to murder and mutiny reads as follows:

'Comrades,

In Germany today the breaking up of the Hitler regime is nearly completed, yet even now the Nazis endeavour with the most reassuring appeals to stir up the women and children against the Allies. But the German people have given up this swindle, and now the Nazi clique must defend their own 'lives after sending millions to their death for the obstinate ideas of one called Hitler.

'Soldiers of the Channel Islands,

Decide now for yourselves what is to be your fate. Hold your arms ready for breaking off with the criminal Nazi officers and their accomplices. Pay attention to the following: When the signal is given for the rebellion, tie a white towel or handkerchief around the left arm and follow the orders of your leaders. On principle, all officers are to be arrested and on resistance shot immediately. N.C.O.'s and men who consider themselves Nazis will be likewise dealt with. Those officers who belong to the rebellion movement will stand by you at the given time with advice and action.

'Non-commissioned Officers,

Follow no longer the false leadership of your officers. Rather rely on your own healthy human understanding.

'Soldiers,

Do not shoot saboteurs; not even those in civilian clothes. Reflect only that every Nazi killed, every munition store blown up, every burnt-down officer's headquarters helps you. Think of the future. Free yourselves through a great deed of liberation.'

The civil population took these agitating happenings very quietly. They knew that they were the work of the German Forces. There was little anxiety for public buildings; for it was regarded as almost certain that the action of those responsible for these sinister events was directed less at the Island or its peoples than at their own officers and at a system with which the men were, for the most part, no longer either in agreement or sympathy. So the public remained perfectly calm, if slightly apprehensive, for owners of requisitioned property, for example, had no means of insurance.

On Sunday, March 18th, the newly arrived General Wolff had a narrow escape. While travelling in the interior of the Island, a bomb was thrown at his motor-car. The bomb missed the window, struck one of the road wheels and failed to explode. It was stated that the soldier responsible for the abortive attempt was promptly arrested and shot. This sufficiently alarming occurrence, taking place so soon after General Wolff's transfer to Jersey, must have administered a rude shock and have conveyed to him and to his staff a broad hint of the dangers surrounding them. It also furnished credible evidence that the intentions laid bare in the second leaflet quoted were outlined in all deadly seriousness.

About the end of March it became known that a second attempt upon the life of General Wolff had been made. Particulars of this were sedulously concealed, even the means adopted being kept secret.

During the evening after the first attempt, a large garage was blown up. It contents, German ammunition and army vehicles, were completely destroyed. Here, fortunately, no life was lost, although damage to surrounding premises was extensive. The explosion was heard and felt over a wide area, and gave rise to some alarm, heightened by the spectacle of columns of smoke and dust rising high into the air, reminiscent of the bombardment of Jersey five years before.

By this time, news from the Western Front could not be

kept from the troops, and its effect upon them became day by day more clearly marked. An unmistakable air of gloomy depression increased as March drew near its close. The war *communiqués*, published in their *Insel Zeitung*, intended as they were to minimise the effect and importance of the Allied offensive, were scanned with contemptuous amusement. The amazing rapidity of the advance of the British and American Armies was followed, by British and Germans alike, with breathless interest which almost overlooked the great Russian successes in the east, vitally important though the latter undoubtedly were.

The first days of April brought Easter. Never before had hope risen so high. The brilliant weather, the inspiringly bright days of early Spring with its opening flowers and budding trees, exercised a cheering influence, and our spirits rose as *communiqué* after *communiqué* daily, even hourly, announced fresh and ever fresh successes. We grudged each security blackout from the British Army front, and, while recognising their necessity, events could not move rapidly enough for us.

Our small but surprisingly efficient crystal receiving sets brought us welcome news from England. At Easter a rousing speech by Mr. Justice du Parcq, himself a Jerseyman of legal eminence, told us that, despite enemy-fostered rumours to the contrary, all was well on the Mainland; that our multitudinous needs were deeply engaging the attention of His Majesty's Government, and that additional help would soon reach us. Somebody else, in the same broadcast, cheered us by saying that London, despite the worst that the Germans had been able to do, was still London; that, on the whole, the main West-End thoroughfares were but little damaged, and that the great shopping centres continued to display wonderful selections of attractive goods and articles, and were daily thronged by eager customers. All this welcome intelligence went to make the Easter of 1945 the best and more hopeful Easter since, five long years before, the German hordes made their first appearance among us.

We began to make plans, always an absorbing occupation. We wondered, after the armistice or the surrender, how long it would be before we should be able to get home again; where we should stay; whom we should find still alive. Then discussion ranged over the burning and urgent question of immediate purchases. Losing all sense of proportion, we awaited the day when we should be able to purchase everything we had lacked for so long, from necessities, such as food, clothes and household goods, to luxuries; from hats to candied peel, from pretty chintzes to curtains, from silver polish to tea services. We were, of course, due for a shock, but much pleasure was derived from anticipation. It was like beginning housekeeping all over again. Jersey was experiencing the nearest approach to relief and happiness that had been felt since the Occupation.

On March 25th, evidently impressed by a deep sense of the growing insecurity of the German position in Jersey, Admiral Hueffmeier delivered a speech in the Forum Picture House in St. Helier to a packed audience convened by order for the purpose. For this occasion the most meticulously careful precautions were observed. The entire building, from roof to cellars, had been carefully searched by picked men of the Field Gendarmerie. For two hours before the arrival of the principal speaker the Forum was surrounded by armed pickets and sentries. No one was allowed to approach, all traffic was diverted, and the men were marched down unarmed.

In an impassioned harangue the Admiral made a clear and unambiguous reply as to his intentions regarding the Channel Islands. Beginning with an appeal for what he called mental preparedness, spiritual and material concentration, he emphasised the difficulties through which all were passing, difficulties which, he felt, would only have the effect of drawing all ranks more closely together and rendering them more worthy of the terrible sacrifices of the Homeland. He pointed out that the military measures taken by the local German Authorities had been such that an attack upon the Channel Islands by the Allied Forces was well within the bounds of possibility. They faced their trial test; they awaited the hour; they prepared themselves for it both spiritually and materially. They were looking forward to meeting the enemy, and it was their task to endure the end before the eyes of a severely tried

Fatherland. They would not allow the Fortress of Jersey to fall into the hands of the adversary. It was their mandate to hold it for the Fuhrer. He was determined to carry out that mandate with all the means at his disposal. With impassioned voice and gesture, the Admiral said: 'I intend to hold out here with you until the Fatherland has won back its lost ground and the final victory is wrested. We do not wish and we cannot allow ourselves to be shamed before the Fatherland which bears a very much heavier burden than any of you.' He assured his hearers that everything was being done, in a spirit of pure National Socialism, to overcome all food difficulties and to create conditions to enable them to hold out indefinitely. 'Passionately filled,' he said in conclusion, 'with belief in the justice of our National Socialist conception of the world in the age breaking upon us, from our present pain and with the certainty of German victory, as Commander of the defences of the Channel Islands I will carry out plainly and without compromise, strictly but justly, the mandate given to me by the Fuhrer. We stand by him, officers and men of the Fortress of Jersey.'

But the troops had neither heart nor stomach for holding the Fortress of Jersey. What they yearned after was food and tobacco and beer; something more to put into their tight-belted bellies than horse-flesh sausage, nettle soup, stolen turnips and rotting potatoes. By this time, their physical condition was pitiable. A high German medical officer, sent over for the express purpose of conducting an inspection with a view to ascertaining what number might be found fit for service elsewhere, had been compelled to report that, of the thousands of men shut up in the Fortress of Jersey, not five per cent. were fit to stand up in the ranks. Death was taking a heavy toll of them. Many had become insane. Tuberculosis had laid its icy hand upon scores, and the remainder, sick to death of the daily duty of turning out on fatigue in search of nettles, sorrel and other wayside ingredients, lounged about the Island the picture of misery and dejection. They knew quite well that Germany had lost the war; that she was well and truly beaten. Few if any had any illusions on that point. All they longed for, apart from creature comforts, was to return home to find out for themselves what had become of their families and their homes, in their absence. They yearned for the end of the war. Many had long ceased to care which side would be successful.

I am convinced that, if in those Spring weeks of 1945 an Allied Force had appeared off Jersey, or a thousand parachute troops had descended upon the Island, the Fortress of Jersey would have fallen into their hands with little or no bloodshed at all. Such was the physical and mental condition of the German troops, I have been assured, that the one thing they looked forward to from day to day was an opportunity to lay down their arms and surrender the Island.

The final days were in turn exciting and disappointing. The Himmler surrender offer was naturally rejected; but expectation that a further offer of unconditional surrender would be made gave way to great disappointment when Doénitz succeeded Hitler. This disappointment was shared by the greater part of the German Occupation Army, which received the news of Hitler's death with resignation. The appointment of a sailor as Fuhrer further angered the men who had been writhing under the command of Admiral Hueffmeier. It was said that an attempt on his life had been made in Guernsey.

During the last few days of the war in Europe, rumour had it that General von Schmettow and Colonel von Helldorf, who had been replaced earlier, had been supporters of the mutinous agitation described, and that it was only because of their removal that a positive revolt had not occurred.

The first few days of May brought thrilling news from the Continent of capitulation after capitulation. Jersey began to buy British flags. Wherever you went you saw people of all ages, singly and in groups, carrying long sticks issuing from paper coverings which quite failed to hide the unmistakable colours of the Union Jack. Some carried them with no covering at all; but nobody paid the slightest attention. A week or two before, agents of the Gestapo, to say nothing of vigilant German officers, would have pounced upon these careless, merry-faced flag-buyers; but now they appeared to have other and weightier matters of which to think. There was a feeling of intense expectancy. All were convinced that the end had come. The only question to which there appeared to be no definite answer was: how soon would the Germans in Jersey realise the hopelessness of their position and hand back the Island?

On Saturday, May 5th, the air, electric as never before, teemed with rumours. At noon, it was said, the Bailiff would announce the German capitulation of Jersey in the Royal Square; loud-speakers had been ordered to be placed in position; all public houses were to be closed and the public confined to their dwellings for forty-eight hours; fatigue parties were clearing obstructions from the runway of the Airport in preparation for American officers, due to arrive by plane to receive the surrender of Jersey on behalf of the British Government; the Bailiff had for hours been in conference with the High Command engaged in settling the terms of the capitulation. These provided that the German officers and troops should remain in their billets and quarters, that they should have full freedom of movement, that they should be fed and rationed at the cost of the States, and that, immediately on the signing of the Peace, they should at once be sent home to Germany; that cars carrying the British flag and full of officers had been seen driving down from the Airport to St. Helier; that the war was at an end.

But there was no word of truth in all this. So much did happen, however, that it is not easy to be precise about the course of events.

On Tuesday, May 8th, came the anxiously awaited notification, in a relayed speech by the Prime Minister, that the surrender of Germany had been signed at Rheims. This great, historic speech was heard in the Royal Square, packed to capacity and suffocation by an enthusiastic crowd of happy people. It came through clearly, every word of Mr. Churchill's well-remembered, distinctly enunciated announcement being heard with perfect distinctness. The statement was punctuated with wild applause. Then, and then only, we knew, beyond the smallest shadow of doubt, that, at long last, the war in Europe was at an end.

We could not realise it. We simply could not take it in.

We left the Royal Square hastily, with but one end in view; to display, without the loss of a moment, every inch of bunting we could beg, borrow or steal. Within an hour the town of St. Helier was gay with flags. In the warm, sunny air of late afternoon, the Union Jack flew out from every flag-staff and from every house. That grand old flag, which had been for so long banished, came into its own. White ensigns, blue ensigns, red ensigns were fluttering wherever you looked, mingling, here and there, with the red-lined saltire of Jersey. By the following morning the decoration of the town was complete. Happy, laughing crowds thronged the streets. The atmosphere was one of care-free holiday. We still had very little food, but nobody cared or thought of that. All we waited for was the arrival of British troops in the King's uniform; to see a British ship once more in Jersey waters.

On Wednesday, May 9th, from an early hour, dense crowds thronged the port and water-front, every eye fixed upon the direction whence the expected warship must make her appearance. There they would have waited throughout the day rather than have returned disappointed to their homes. At length there came a burst of cheering and loud cries of 'There she is' as, rounding Noirmont Point, the grey hull and twin funnels of His Majesty's Flotilla Leader *Beagle* came steaming majestically to her anchorage beyond Elizabeth Castle, the white ensign of the Royal Navy flying out in the morning breeze. I think that that was the moment at which we realised, at which it came home to us, that the long years of German domination were over; that we were once more free.

Individual reaction to extreme joy provides an interesting study for the observant psychologist. Just as, in the Royal Square on the preceding day, Mr. Churchill's sympathetic utterances moved many of his hearers to unconcealed and unconcealable emotion, so the arrival of a comparatively insignificant British naval unit affected many of those who witnessed it in a similar manner. Laughter and echoing cheers there were in plenty; but many who saw a British ship, for the first time after so many years, were fain furtively to wipe away happy tears of which they need in no way to have been ashamed.

When, some time later, the *Beagle*'s picket-boat came ashore with two officers in uniform, the fervour and enthusiasm of the crowd's welcome were such that the greatest difficulty was experienced in extricating them from such an amount of hearty back-slapping, hand-shaking and merciless pressure as threatened at times to result in personal injury. Amidst roar after roar of delirious cheering, the welcome visitors at length reached a waiting car and, as it crawled at a snail's pace through the masses of excited people who pressed up to and even mounted the running-boards, the panting occupants were compelled to stand and shake dozens of hands through the windows. Soon, however, the car was forced to a standstill, the pressure and density of the crowd rendering further progress impossible, and, finally, the two officers were plucked forcibly from it and, showered with flowers, carried shoulder-high to the office of the Harbour Master, where, appearing at one of the windows, they were greeted by more vociferous cheering and a thunderous rendering of the National Anthem. How they finally escaped is not recorded; but, a little later, an officer and party of men of the Hampshire Regiment came ashore from the *Beagle* and were accorded a similar rapturous reception.

Nobody living in Jersey will ever forget that wonderful May 9th. On that historic day the people saw at last the men who had become to them almost beings of fable. St. Helier gave itself up to celebrations such as the Island had never before witnessed. Every man, woman and child became a centre of whole-hearted joy to themselves as well as an unending fountain of adulation to their deliverers. Countless voices sang and shrilled, a swirling sea of exultancy swelled and swept madly, rising to mighty waves of acclaim. Before, beside and behind the incoming warriors, the crowds pushed and struggled and fought for a handshake, heedless of the motor traffic which at times threatened life and limb. As new arrivals made their appearance, the crowds rushed to greet them, drunk with the ecstasy of their newly-regained freedom, great eddies in a vast, irresistible whirling tide of joy. These were not only our liberators, they were the Men of Marathon who had won what may well prove to have been civilisation's final battle; men of great armies to whom the shadow of swift-moving doom gave but increased power and tenacity such as inspired the hosts of Cyrus and Cambyses. They were, in a word, men of our own blood and kin, the soldiers of Britain. Small wonder, then, that we lost our heads; this day, of all the days in her history, was Jersey's Great Day.

There landed a detachment of the Hampshires, with details drawn from other distinguished Regiments, as well as from the Royal Artillery, Royal Army Service Corps, and other units. They were speedily marched to temporary quarters in adjacent hotels previously occupied by German troops.

In the meantime, on board the *Beagle*, which carried Rear Admiral C. Stuart, Brigadier A. E. Snow, appointed to command the British troops in the Channel Islands, and other officers, arrangements were in course of completion for taking over the Island of Jersey from the Germans. General Wolff, Commander of the German troops, was summoned on board, where he received his orders which were confirmed later in the day on shore. At this latter interview with Colonel N. V. A. Robinson, the officer detailed to command in Jersey, General Wolff was directed to see that, by six o'clock that evening, the town of St. Helier, the port, and the entire southern portion of the Island were cleared of German troops, who were to be disarmed and ordered to deposit their arms and ammunition in certain specified *dépôts*. By nightfall, therefore, German uniforms, so long a loathsome eyesore to Jersey people, had completely disappeared from the streets of St. Helier.

The surrender of the Channel Islands had already officially taken place off Guernsey.

The two British ships which had been despatched for the duty of securing the surrender of the Channel Islands, H.M.S. *Beagle* and H.M.S. *Bulldog*, made their landfall off Guernsey on Tuesday, May 8th, reaching an agreed spot about four miles off St. Peter Port Harbour. After considerable delay, a very old trawler, flying the German flag, was seen approaching. Coming within hail of the British ships, she lowered a rubber dinghy into which an officer and several ratings descended. The sea being rather choppy, the somewhat junior officer, Kapitan Leutnant Zimmerman, presented a drenched and dishevelled appearance as he climbed aboard the *Bulldog*.

In the presence of Brigadier Snow, the German, on being informed that unconditional surrender of the Channel Islands was demanded, vehemently disclaimed any authority to complete such an arrangement, and stated that his mission was to ascertain, for the consideration of his superiors, 'the terms of the armistice.'

He was thereupon promptly and curtly informed that there could be no question of 'armistice,' but one of complete and unconditional surrender only. He then communicated to the Brigadier, with every appearance of apprehensive misgiving, that he had received instructions to say that the British ships must quit their present anchorage, where their continued presence would be looked upon as 'an unfriendly act'. He was shortly afterwards handed the irreducible terms of the British demand. Kapitan Leutnant Zimmerman went ashore with this document. The ships then got up anchor and quitted the vicinity of St. Peter Port, as it was felt that neighbouring batteries of heavy guns might possibly render the anchorage chosen somewhat unhealthy.

At the time fixed, one minute after midnight of Tuesday, May 8th, the two warships arrived at a new rendezvous. Again there was an appreciable delay. At length, the lights of the dilapidated trawler were seen. Soon after, a boat was put over her side and Kapitan Leutnant Zimmermen, accompanied by the notorious Major General Heine, stepped on board the *Bulldog* and were received by Brigadier Snow.

Standing stiffly at attention, General Heine replied affirmatively and satisfactorily to the questions of the Brigadier and, at seven o'clock on the morning of Wednesday, May 9th, the formal article of surrender of the Channel Islands were duly signed, it is said, on an up-ended empty rum cask on the *Bulldog*'s quarter deck, an act which brought five years of grinding German occupation to a final and overdue end.

Saturday, May 12th, in Jersey, was given over to the people as a public holiday and day of rejoicing. The brilliant weather continued; and from an early hour, while British planes of various types roared unceasingly overhead, an immense concourse of people thronged the port and the roadway running round St. Aubin's Bay, watching, with deeply thrilled interest which never for one moment abated, the arrival in the Island of bodies of British troops. On the following day, disembarkation of more troops and stores continued from a number of transport and supply-ships which, with several large tank-landing-craft, conveyed quantities of provisions and stores both for the troops and the islanders. As the ships discharged their cargoes and got ready for sea, large bodies of German prisoners were embarked for destinations in the United Kingdom, their departure being witnessed by the Island people with dignified calm. There were no demonstrations.

Great and wonderful was the transformation. Where yesterday there was only misery, to-day there were only smiles. Everything was joyful, from the unbroken May sunshine to the coloured flags. Electricity and the telephone service were at once restored. Potatoes were still scarce, but bread became abundant. As if by some miracle motor-cars, hidden for five years, made a sudden appearance. Everything German disappeared, from their currency to their restrictions.

At first only postcards, specially printed for the purpose, could be sent to the United Kingdom; but on the 18th, full postal and telegraphic communication was finally restored.

The rush was terrific. It was difficult, by reason of the crowds, eager once more to avail themselves of postal facilities, to penetrate into the Post Office at all. For days, long queues of hundreds of people waited patiently hour by hour, telegram in hand, to pass their messages through the *guichet* to the one solitary official who was all the Jersey Postmaster could see his way to provide. But, as one person philosophically observed: 'Oh, well, we've waited for five years to get news from home; I suppose we can wait a few days longer.'

The Germans had gone or were gradually going; our splendid troops were in our midst; we were free once more to live

147

our own lives in our own way. No longer, all apprehensively, did we take up the German-directed *Evening Post* and scan its columns for more and ever more oppressive orders of the Hun Platzkommandantur. No longer did we glance timorously round in search of Gestapo agents who might be lurking to overhear our conversations in the street. All fear of sudden expulsion from our homes to make way for German occupants was removed. The daily and nightly anxieties which, for five long years had harassed us by day and so often rendered our nights a sleepless torment had passed away for ever. Relief, gratitude, happiness had taken the place of those nightmares of the past. Freedom from a hated foreign thraldom was ours at last, and how we appreciated it!

APPENDIX

(A)

English Translation of the Oath as Civil Governor Administered to Mr. A. M. Coutanche by the Lieutenant Bailiff of Jersey, Mr. P. de C. Le Cornu, on June 21st, 1940.

Since it has pleased God to call you to the Office of Lieutenant Governor of the Island of Jersey, you swear and promise here in the Presence of God that you will faithfully fulfil the said office under our Sovereign Lord King George the Sixth, by the Grace of God, of Great Britain, of Ireland and of the British Dominions beyond the Seas, King, Emperor of India, renouncing all other Foreign Sovereignty and protecting his Rights. You will aid and defend all Jurisdictions, Privileges, Distinctions and Authorities appertaining to His Majesty as also all Liberties, Rights, Dignities, Laws, Customs and Privileges of the said Island with the Welfare of the Public and the advancement of the same. Item. You will lend your strength (to ensure) that His Majesty's Justice be revered and obeyed, and His Judgements and Ordinances daily executed, opposing all Traitors, Murderers, Thieves, Rioters, Mutineers and Seditious Persons so that Power reside in the King. All this you promise upon your conscience.

(B)

Memorandum containing proposals for securing more adequate and more regular supplies of food and other necessaries for the Civil Population of the Channel Islands.

The supply of food-stuffs to the Channel Islands is a matter which for some months past has given occasion for anxiety, as existing sources of purchase have displayed indications of something approaching precariousness. The question, therefore, has been carefully considered as to whether it might not be possible to arrange for shipments of provisions and other necessaries to reach these Islands with regularity and in such quantities as to abate the unhappy privation which has so long prevailed. It is in the hope that some such scheme as that hereinafter outlined may prove capable of arrangement that this Memorandum has been drawn up. It is, of course, fully realised that, to the initiation of any future plans of *ravitaillement*, the consent and concurrence of the German Authorities must be obtained; and in order to assist in the realisation of that necessity, the following clear-cut precedent may with confidence be cited.

In the month of October, 1914, the Kingdom of Belgium, then almost wholly in German occupation, was threatened with famine. Crops everywhere had failed or been destroyed. Stores of food of all descriptions, due to the vast requisitions of the German Military Authorities for the immense armies passing through the country, had shrunk almost to vanishing point. At length, the American Minister to Belgium, Mr. Brand Whitlock, realising with great foresight the gravity of the impending peril, approached the Governor-General of the occupied territories, Field Marshal Baron von der Goltz, and offered, subject to the latter's acceptance, to obtain from the United States, then a neutral country, regular shipments of necessaries to Belgium in sufficient quantities finally to remove all fear of future food shortage. An English translation of the Field Marshal's letter on the subject is attached hereto. From this it will be seen that not only did he at once agree to the Minister's proposals, but, of equal importance, guaranteed that the food to be imported for the Belgian people should be free from all German requisition and reserved exclusively for those for whom it was intended. This undertaking, it should be noted, was scrupulously observed. These facts, easily substantiated, would appear to afford exceptionally valuable

150

material in discussing a similar arrangement with those German Authorities to whose hands the destinies of the civil population of the Channel Islands have been committed.

The proposal which the writer would suggest is that, with German concurrence as stated, arrangements be made through the Portuguese Embassy or Legation in France for shipments of necessary food-stuffs to be supplied to Jersey and Guernsey from the Republic of Portugal. The Portuguese seaport of Leixoes is only about 700 miles from Jersey; from there, small freighters of the Companhia Nacional de Navigacao, for which safe-conducts could be obtained, could reach Jersey in about three days, and these vessels would have no difficulty in entering the harbours of St. Helier or St. Peter Port.

The wealth and importance of the resources of Portugal are much greater than most persons suppose. The country and its people are well known to the writer who, due to an intimate knowledge, both of them and of their language, has learned to regard them with both admiration and esteem. Their sympathy for Britain and the British people is boundless, and it may be accepted as a certainty that, once aware of our needs, they would spare no effort to remove the difficulties which at present surround us.

The first question which naturally arises is: With what can Portugal supply us? The following is the answer: wheat, barley, oat-flour, rye and maize. Olives, oranges, lemons, figs and almonds. Canned, preserved and dried fruit. Meat both fresh and preserved, also dried fish of various kinds, hams and bacon. Eggs in abundance. Olive oil for cooking. Coffee and sugar from the Portuguese Colonies in Africa. Tobacco, cigars and cigarettes. Wines and brandy. Coal. Manufactured goods such as boots and shoes of excellent quality, together with silk, woollen and cotton fabrics. The foregoing are but a few of the many articles which Portugal could supply, and which her shippers would gladly furnish to these Islands in abundance.

Payment for such supplies is a matter which, it can be confidently assumed, need occasion the Channel Islands little anxiety. From the earliest days of the German Occupation, both in Parliament and in messages to the Islands, His Majesty's Government have expressed their deep regret at the temporary withdrawal of their protection and their profound sympathy with the Island people in an experience as painful as it has been unavoidable. There can be little doubt that, in view of the privation of which some 60,000 British subjects have been the victims, His Majesty's Treasury would unhesitatingly bear the cost of the provisions and necessities supplied. Even in the improbable contingency of their refusal, it can be accepted as certain that they would advance the cost in the form of a loan or grant-in-aid repayable without interest over a great number of years.

The method whereby the proposed arrangement could be set on foot is a matter of great simplicity, and could be dealt with later.

Such, in brief outline, is the proposal which is offered for consideration. It is one which would appear to have everything to recommend it. It is difficult to imagine what objection, fairly considered, the German Authorities could find to oppose, more especially due to the fact that, should present sources of supply fail, under the provisions of The Hague Convention the cost of maintaining the populations of the Channel Islands would undoubtedly fall upon them. Jersey, December 17th, 1941.

Translation of a letter addressed by the Governor-General of Belgium to the American Minister at Brussels accepting the latter's proposals for the revictualling of the country.

Brussels, October 16th, 1914

In accordance with your esteemed letter of this date, I have the honour to confirm that I approve with a lively satisfaction the work of the Comité Central de Secours et d'alimentation, and that I do not hesitate to give formally and expressly by these presents the assurance that food-stuffs of all kinds imported by the Comité for the feeding of the civilian population of Belgium will be reserved exclusively for the needs of the population of Belgium, that conse-quently these food-stuffs are exempt from requisition on the part of the Military Authorities, and that they remain at the exclusive disposition of the Comité.

(Signed)   Fhr. von de Goltz,
Field Marshal General.

(C)

The following is a translation of a description of the occupation of Jersey published for German consumption by a person describing himself as Sonderfuehrer Hans Auerbach, who must either have been seriously misinformed or a lineal descendant of Ananias.

HOW A YOUNG LIEUTENANT TOOK THE ISLAND OF JERSEY

On July 1st, 1940, the German wireless announced that the Channel Islands had been occupied by a bold stroke of the Air Force. It is of interest to record the true facts of the occupation. This incident of the war will be of value at a later date as it was through this operation that British soil in Europe, for the first time, was occupied by German troops.

From Normandy, from Cape Carteret or Cape de la Hogue, the Channel Islands appear grey shadows between the horizon and the sea, shadows which in hazy weather disappear. What do they conceal? The telescopes of Coast Guards were continually fixed upon them, as this was England; this was the last bastion turned towards Europe after she had been driven from the Continent. Headquarters were, therefore, very much interested in the Islands, as they greatly desired to know what was happening in them. Rumour had it that they had been completely evacuated. Reconnaissance undertook to discover the true state of affairs.

On June 30th, Lieutenant Kern flew over the Islands for that purpose. He saw Guernsey with its glass-houses; he saw apparently inhospitable Alderney, the small Island of Sark, and then he turned to the largest Island of Jersey. He flew over the beaches and harbours, over small estates and villages until he reached St. Helier. The streets of the town were almost deserted. The Island seemed dead. Finally, after close investigation people were discernible. They emerged cautiously from the air raid shelters and gazed curiously upward. There was, therefore, still life in Jersey. The most important fact was that it could be reported to the General that there was no sign of defence.

On the second flight, the machine met three planes of similar type from the sister Squadron. They were flying towards Guernsey and, as was later made known, that morning they occupied the Island.

In the meantime, the English must have smelt a rat for they sent two Blenheims over the Channel. They met three Dornier Fighters near Guernsey, and Lieutenant Forster was able to shoot them both down with one reconnaissance plane.

As a result of the information obtained, the General decided to call upon Jersey to surrender. It was two o'clock in the morning when the summons, signed by the General, reached the Squadron. There were three summonses each for Jersey and Guernsey all in the same terms. As it was a letter of parley, the usual coloured pouch could not be used; pouches were, therefore, cut from the bed-linen belonging to the Captain of the French Squadron whose deserted quarters had been taken over by the German Squadron. It was still dark when the machine started for Jersey.

The Island was reached in the early hours. Once more a German plane was droning over Jersey. Only a few islanders were up, but the pouch containing the summons to surrender which had been dropped was soon found and taken to the Authorities. Later, it was recounted in the Island how surprised the dreamy town of St. Helier was to receive such an early visit.

After dropping the summons the plane returned, and the General awaited signs of surrender. It can be imagined how tense the German airmen were during the period of waiting. The General had stipulated that, as a sign of surrender, white flags should be flown. There could be no peace of mind until

154

the undertaking had been carried to a successful conclusion.

Wild rumours were running through the Services. According to these an English cruiser was supposed to have made its appearance in the vicinity of Jersey. In order to clear up this point, Lieutenant Kern was sent back to the Islands. He arrived without being attacked, and could see nothing of any active defence. The Island lay there as peacefully as on the previous day. Then, as the machine flew over the beaches and gardens and town, an idea came to the Lieutenant. He saw life going on peacefully below him; he saw the beautiful Island and he had been ordered to bring back accurate information. As he flew towards the Airport and saw the beautifully situated landing ground with its elegant white buildings, he made his decision.

He would take Jersey.

The plane banked over the flying field. He gave the order to land. What were the sensations of the crew? If the field were mined, then it would be all over. If there were means of defence, it would not be much better for them. But if things went smoothly, and no one doubted but that they would, then they would be the first Germans to set foot on British soil. Lonely the machine rolled over the ground. The Lieutenant strode towards the Administration Building, followed by the plane which was to secure the way into the unknown—with its machine gun ready.

Nothing happened. Finally, from the Airport Building, emerged an excited man who, to the astonishment of the newcomers, spoke German. He took the Lieutenant to the telephone and got in touch with the Bailiff.

Yes, the Bailiff had received the summons to surrender.

Why were the white flags not flying?

Because the Bailiff had to wait for the decision of the States, and the States had in the meantime agreed to unconditional surrender.

The Bailiff requested that the General should be informed to that effect.

Lieutenant Kern informed the Bailiff that the Island was under German occupation.

Shortly afterwards, the planes which had been sent for from the Squadron appeared. They were packed with men. While these machines were appearing over the Island, the white flags were beginning to be flown.

It was a strange sight that met the gaze of the Germans flying under the blue sky of that Summer's day. That of a pleasant town from which every kind of white, from sheets to pocket handkerchiefs, was flying.

When the Captain of the Squadron landed, the Bailiff, the Government Secretary, and the Chief of Police were waiting to receive him at the Airport. The surrender was concluded in short time, the British officials maintaining a correct attitude. Here also the relations between the Troops of Occupation and the local Authorities have not deteriorated. The first orders were given by the Captain. The men who came over in the first machines took over the apparatus used for communication, the rate of exchange was fixed, and a curfew ordered for the Island. The Germans then drove in waiting cars to St. Helier, being stared at on the way by the policemen and the population. It all happened so naturally that it seemed the Squadron had nothing else to do in the war but to occupy the Channel Islands.

The strokes of the Air Force are audacious and swift. The English have felt them continually, ever since they refused the hand of peace held out to them by the Fuhrer. Swift action brought the Island of Jersey into German hands with a speed not held to be possible by the experience of history.

The next morning, to the pride of the Air Force, a Swastika Flag, *sewn by the inhabitants of the Island*, was hoisted into the blue ether.

(D)

Mr. Trevor J. Matthews's Letter to the Jersey Evening Post, *dated June 24th, 1940.*

Sir,—Many people appear to be gravely concerned as to what their financial position would be in the event of a cessation of communication with the Mainland whence most dividends, interest, pensions, etc., come to us. Fear of penury through lack of such receipts has caused people to leave the Island and others to exist in a state of nervousness, which is, in my opinion, undesirable and unnecessary.

I would suggest that, in the circumstances, we should be in a state of 'closed economy' where the banks would, in their own interest, provide adequate finance to keep the wheels turning. Thus, where they know that a client had an income and assets prevented from transfer to Jersey, they would advance suitable amounts to meet his cost of living; the client's expenditure would return to the banks through the tradesmen who would receive the money. Every advance would create a corresponding deposit, and there would be no strain on the local finances of the banks. Obviously, if the banks did not adopt such measures, there would be a general suspension of payments which would be injurious to the banks as to everybody else.

Another error prevailing in some quarters is the supposition that money deposited at the banks might be seized in the event of invasion and that it is better to withdraw it in notes. It should, however, be realised that a bank deposit is only a row of figures which clearly could not be seized by anybody and, in a closed economy, represents only a call on a corresponding amount of local goods and services (which an invader would requisition directly if he wanted them).

Withdrawal of money in the form of notes is undesirable unless required for expenditure—as the holder runs the risk of loss, destruction and theft. Notes, after all, are only pieces of paper, no safer and more destructible than a bank deposit.

The interests of all call for as little disturbance of normal methods as circumstances permit. Tradesmen and others should continue to give reasonable credit to reliable customers, employees should not be dismissed unless they can find work, payments should be made punctually and preferably by cheque. Economy in purchase of goods is necessary as we do not know when supplies may be interrupted, and every effort should be made to grow more food. This question of supplies is important and, in comparison, the problems of money and credit (the means of distribution and supply) are easy to solve.

It should be emphasised that my remarks have reference to a special contingency, and are not necessarily to be taken as of general application.

TREVOR J. MATTHEWS

THE END

**Give them
the pleasure of choosing**

Book Tokens can be bought
and exchanged at most
bookshops in Great Britain
and Ireland.

WAR FICTION AND
NON-FICTION FROM NEL